winning fencing

winning fencing

Marvin Nelson

with Rick Reiff

Henry Regnery Company·Chicago

Library of Congress Cataloging in Publication Data

Nelson, Marvin.
    Winning fencing.

    Bibliography: p. 167
    1. Fencing   I. Reiff, Rick, joint author.
II. Title.
GV1147.N44   796.8'6   75-13235
ISBN 0-8092-8335-2
ISBN 0-8092-8334-4 pbk.

Photography by Dennis Weeks

Copyright © 1975 by Marvin Nelson and Rick Reiff
All rights reserved
Published by Henry Regnery Company
          180 North Michigan Avenue
          Chicago, Illinois 60601
Manufactured in the United States of America
Library of Congress Catalog Card Number: 75-13235
International Standard Book Number: 0-8092-8335-2 (cloth)
                                 0-8092-8334-4 (paper)
Published simultaneously in Canada by
          Fitzhenry & Whiteside Limited
          150 Lesmill Road
          Don Mills, Ontario M3B 2T5
          Canada

Cover photograph: Photographed in
Shakespearean Garden, The Art Institute of
Chicago. Fencer: Edwin Longstreet, Jr.
Photographer: Dennis Weeks.

acknowledgments

My thanks to Robert G. Ostrowski, fencing coach at the University of Chicago, and to Edwin Longstreet, Jr., my former students, for posing for the photographs in this book. I would also like to thank Charles Schmitter, professor of physical education and head fencing coach at Michigan State University in East Lansing for his encouragement, suggestions, and advice, especially in the chapter dealing with épée.

contents

appendixes

preface

Welcome to the world of fencing. It's a big world, large enough to accommodate the tastes and the athletic interests of many different enthusiasts.

One segment of this world considers fencing an ancient art, having its beginnings before recorded history and an evolution parallel to the history of mankind. For another segment, it is a modern, dynamic sport in which contestants vie against one another for personal glory and the honor of their countries in the Olympic Games. For a third group, fencing is simply an enjoyable sport, a recreation that supplies the excitement of man-to-man combat but in complete safety.

In this book, I will try to share with you the fundamental techniques and strategies of fencing as they have developed over the years and as I have learned and experienced them. The book will provide a basic source of instruction for both beginners and developing fencers; text and illustrations are based on classical form and style.

This is an age of world travel and it is comforting to know that as a fencer you will find instant friends among fencers almost anywhere—from Nairobi to Hong Kong and Tokyo, from New Orleans to London, Paris, Tel Aviv, and Cairo.

This international sport could also prove to be an important factor in producing greater understanding, and something more than tolerance between men of differing colors, creeds, and cultures. Actually, fencers participate in many international competitions and with much less dissension than exists in most sports and with a free and easy exchange of ideas. Indeed, the brotherhood of the sword is truly a closely knit fraternity, without confrontation, just hard and intense competition. It is, in a word, a great sport.

chapter one

The history of fencing—more than the genealogy of an art and sport—provides a thread of history itself, for it has closely paralleled the story of civilization. Fencing actually has its origins in prehistory. The first time a man delivered blows to his prey, pursuer, or fellow man, he was fencing, albeit crudely. And the first swords, like most early implements, were chipped into shape from flint found in chalk and limestone.

With the discovery of the malleability of bronze, metal swords were produced. However, these early weapons were too flexible to be made very long, and they chipped and notched easily. Man learned to temper hot iron by inserting it in water to make longer and better swords. By the time of the Middle Ages, skilled craftsmen kept their formulas a closely guarded secret. Magical powers were also believed to pervade the tempering process.

a brief history of fencing

Though the history of fencing closely parallels that of combat, there is some evidence that ancient civilizations also developed sporting varieties. A relief carving in the temple near Luxor, Egypt, built around 1200 B.C., shows what is almost certainly a fencing bout. The fencers are wearing masks and using swords with protective tips. There are also spectators, a jury, and other officials. A hieroglyphic inscription on the sculpture has one fencer saying, "On guard and admire what my valiant hand shall do."

However, in ancient Greece, fencing was not a part of the Olympic Games first celebrated in 776 B.C. *Oplomachia*, a sport similar to fencing, was probably restricted to training warriors, not for leisure. Roman gladiators were taught the use of swords and other weapons in schools called *ludi* (the earliest known fencing schools) by instructors called *lanestae*.

3

In the early Middle Ages, when barbarians overran Europe, every soldier was equipped with a sword and versed in its use. Duels became an acceptable and common means of settling differences. Knights, to maintain their skills in peacetime, engaged in jousts on horseback. Refined swordwork, however, was unknown. Heavy, unwieldy weapons were needed to crack and bludgeon armor-clad foes. The clash of sword and armor became an escalating battle: as armor became more impenetrable, swords became heavier and their use more primitive.

When swords were bypassed for more effective weapons in the mid-fourteenth century, their use became more refined. And by the fifteenth century, guilds like the Marxbruder in Germany, were springing up across Europe to instruct soldiers and gentlemen in the nuances of swordplay. Teachers became famous for their "secret strokes"—really just orthodox fencing movements previously unemployed. In the late fifteenth and early sixteenth century, fencing books began to circulate throughout Europe.

The Italians became expert in the use of the light, beautifully balanced rapier, with the unarmed hand used to parry and usually holding a dagger, cloak, or buckler (a small shield). Opponents stood almost square to each other and circled around for better position. As the style developed, Italians discarded most of the popular wrestling techniques, discovered the lunge and introduced the duck (passata sotto) and sidestep (in quartata).

Early in the seventeenth century, the button-tip on the sword was introduced and the convention of right-of-way—which made fencing a game of alternating action (attack and defense)—was established. As a result, fencing became safer. The invention of the mask by La Boessiere in 1780 finally allowed for a virtually injury-free bout. Techniques and strategy improved remarkably.

Since the sophisticated movements of this developing sport were almost useless to the gentleman dueling an opponent who brandished a heavier, more lethal, weapon, the épée was introduced. The heavier épée, heavier than the rapier and later tee foil, became the dueling weapon. When training for a duel, an épée fencer often wore no mask or protective padding.

At the end of the seventeenth century, the change in men's

fashions prompted by the court of Louis XIV of France necessitated a still lighter and more maneuverable blade: the fleuret (foil), which was also an item of dress. Rapier fencing gave way to swift and refined swordplay in which parries were made with the blade rather than the left hand.

In the early nineteenth century, a relative of the Oriental scimitar, the sabre, became the national weapon of Hungary. The Italians introduced a lighter sabre which became popular in both bouts and duels. The Hungarians then regained the initiative and produced a superior school of light sabre fencing. However, it was an Italian master, Italo Santelli, who systematized Hungarian sabre work, and he is still honored in Hungary as a national hero.

By the dawn of the twentieth century, fencing was a full-fledged sport. There were both épée and sabre competition at the revival of the Olympics in 1896, and more events were added in later games. National fencing organizations were formed in Great Britain in 1902 and France in 1906. The United States did not have a fencing school until 1874, and the Amateur Fencers League of America was established in 1891.

During the first half of the twentieth century, fencing in foil and épée was dominated by the Italians and French; Hungarians led in the sabre. However, Eastern European countries, especially the Soviet Union and Hungary with some exceptions, moved to the forefront in all forms of fencing by the mid-1950s. Their new style capitalized on the introduction of electric scoring devices that could detect touches previously unnoticed by human judges. Eastern European fencers abandoned many of the classical techniques and emphasized instead speed and mobility. As a result, many international champions are young men and women, a phenomenon once unheard of. Fencing is no longer a matter of history. Rather, it is taking its place on the list of exciting and expanding sports.

chapter two

The recent growth of interest in all kinds of sports, participatory and spectator, has been phenomenal. Fencing became one of the beneficiaries of this trend and is attracting a larger and more diverse following than ever before. An increasing number of communities—park and recreation districts, high schools, and colleges—are sponsoring programs in fencing. Attendance by persons from all walks of life, with a wide disparity in age and physical endowment, has exceeded expectations.

Although I have engaged in almost every competitive sport, I know of no other that offers as many rewards to the participant than fencing. I have been told by fencing masters who also play jai alai that fencing can match it in speed. Fencing increases not only physical but also mental responses to such a degree that it has been called "chess on wheels." Its nature is such that most of its

6

the start-up

followers are satisfied with only a moderate degree of proficiency. These skills often enable the fencer to have a more active physical and mental life in advancing years. Even some blind persons are now learning to fence—sharpening and refining their other senses, having fun and healthful exercise at the same time.

AMATEUR FENCERS LEAGUE OF AMERICA

The Amateur Fencers League of America (AFLA) has played an important part in the growth of fencing. This nonprofit, tax-exempt organization is the official governing body for fencing activities in the United States and is recognized by the U.S. Olympic

7

First position of salute   Second position of salute

Committee and the International Fencing Federation (FIE). Its divisions are geographically distributed for the convenience of its members.

As a beginner, you are urged to join the AFLA. Its officials are eager to interest new people in the sport, and members, too, are always willing to render assistance to individuals, groups, or clubs. The official magazine, *American Fencing*, is published six times a year, with much information and articles submitted by novices and well-known fencing masters.

EQUIPMENT*

To begin fencing, you will need a foil, a wire-mesh mask, a fencing

---

*Relevant sections from the AFLA Rule Book are presented in appendix A. Refer to them for exact specifications on all equipment.

Third position of salute. The third position of the salute is made first to opponents, then officials. It is from this position that the fencer comes to guard and puts his mask on so that he is ready to respond to the Director.

glove with gauntlet for your sword hand, and the specified protective jacket. Sweat shirts or tee shirts are neither adequate nor safe. Fencing trousers are not required unless you fence in competition. There are shoes made especially for fencing, but any good tennis or deck shoe will suffice.

If you are part of a group of beginning fencers, it is wise to order items in quantity, because suppliers are likely to give you a discount. Some clubs require three bids on substantial orders. If a mistake is made in an order, as occasionally happens, simply return the equipment and restate your order. I have never known a supplier to hesitate on correcting a wrong order.

Clothing

Jackets, gloves, and foils are made for either right- or left-handed fencers. Be certain to specify handedness correctly. Suppliers of

9

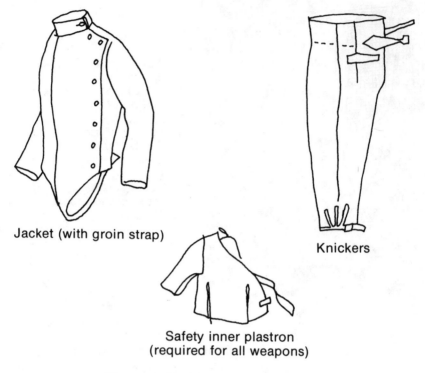

Jacket (with groin strap)

Knickers

Safety inner plastron
(required for all weapons)

Figure 1. Clothing used for fencing

fencing equipment (see Appendix G) are usually happy to send you a catalog that will indicate how to measure for correct jacket and trouser sizes, for waist-length jackets or those with groin straps.

Fencing gloves are made of various leathers, ranging from brown suede to white kidskin, and vary in price. Jackets and trousers are always white, usually made of duck or sail cloth. Stretch nylon cloth has become popular but is more expensive. (The fencers in our photographs are wearing uniforms made of nylon.) Fencing clothing varies in weight, design, and thickness. They are fastened with either button, zipper, or Velcro closures. Garments for women must be so specified because they are designed to meet their special protective needs. Sabre jackets require

10

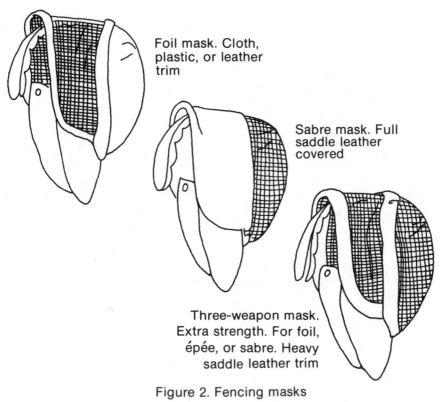

Foil mask. Cloth, plastic, or leather trim

Sabre mask. Full saddle leather covered

Three-weapon mask. Extra strength. For foil, épée, or sabre. Heavy saddle leather trim

Figure 2. Fencing masks

extra padding or thickness and are usually of waist length.

Mask

Masks are made for foil, for foil and épée, or with a heavier mesh, for sabre only. Heavier "three-weapon" masks are made for fencers who fence in competition with all three weapons. Foil and foil-épée masks are made with white or black cloth trim; the sabre mask has leather trim in white or saddle color, covering top and sides. The bib or protective throat piece is always white and may be either plastic or cloth, sewn in place or with snaps for easy removal and washing. I would suggest a mask with the sewn-in

11

cloth bib; it is possible that a rule change will be made requiring sewn-in bibs because they offer more protection.

Always wear a mask when fencing, even when you are "working on something" with a partner or just "horsing around." Never take a playful jab at another fencer without a mask. An inexperienced fencer may instinctively react to your "threat" with a parry and return the jab, and *you* could get hurt. The experienced swordsman will react with a parry and riposte—because he has been taught to do so.

If you use protective equipment at all times and demand the same from your opponents, fencing can be a very safe sport. I have never had an accident in all my years as a coach, nor have my students, because I have insisted on the proper use of equipment.

RULES AND RIGHT OF WAY

One of the first things to do is to obtain a rule book (the AFLA will gladly send you one for $3.00). Always have it with you when you fence to settle arguments; it is the primary source for rule information. Read the sections dealing with *right of way* first. This rule provides for an orderly system of play, and makes fencing a game of alternating action. It is this rule that maintains the identity of the foil and distinguishes it from fencing with the épée. Basically, a fencer has the right of way when he extends his arm and continuously threatens his opponent's valid target as shown in the photo. In other words, he has the attack. The opponent must make a defensive move called a parry before he can follow with a counteraction called the riposte. The aggressor then parries the riposte and makes another offensive action.

When two fencers conceive an attack simultaneously so that the director cannot decide who was first in point of time, he declares that neither has the right of way. In this situation, the two fencers are placed on guard again and the bout continues.

This rule was especially important before the invention of the mask. It prohibited fencers from attacking each other at the same time and thus impaling themselves. With this rule and the invention of the mask, chances of injury were greatly reduced and fencers were free to innovate, expand their technique, and improve their tactical game.

There is no right of way, however, in épée. An épée bout bears more resemblance to the legendary duels than does foil fencing. In fact, épée has been referred to as the realistic weapon.

THE BOUT

The bout is the unit of competition—one fencer against another. Bouts won or lost determine, in the preliminary round of a competition, the fencers who will "go up" to the next round and then the order of placement in succeeding rounds and in the final round.

Each bout in men's foil is for five touches—the bout ends when one fencer has been touched five times: in women's foil, a bout ends with four touches. The fencer receiving the fewest touches is the victor. The duration of play is six minutes for men and five minutes for women. The time between "halts" is deducted by a timer. A photographer's darkroom clock or a stopwatch is used. The score and time are kept by a designated official or officials. The rules of a competition are published in advance on a printed AFLA schedule or announced at the beginning. The number of entries will determine the number of fencers in each pool. For example, with forty-eight entries, there would be eight pools of six fencers each, or six pools of eight fencers each. This might depend upon how many qualified officials are available for presiding on the strips, the areas where each pool is being fenced. Very likely, the first three fencers in each pool will advance to the next round.

With eight pools, for instance, twenty-four fencers would remain after the others had been eliminated. In the event of ties, officials make a decision based on touches given and on touches received. Eight fencers from the next round would then be eligible to fence in the final round. A precise method is contained in the

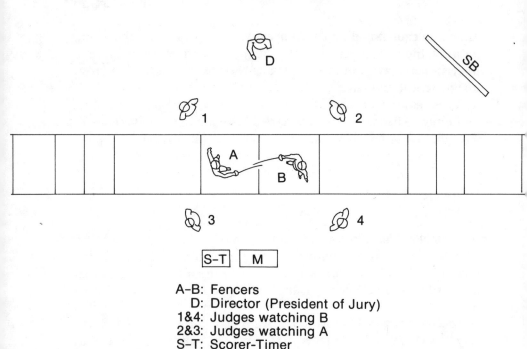

A–B: Fencers
 D: Director (President of Jury)
1&4: Judges watching B
2&3: Judges watching A
S–T: Scorer-Timer
 M: Electric Machine
SB: Scoreboard

Figure 3. The positions occupied by the jury and competitors.

rule book under the heading "Indicators."

Bouts are scored on an official AFLA scoresheet. The names appear in the order in which the officials have determined the seeding, or the quality of the fencers if known. This may be determined on reputation at times or on the official classification an individual fencer has received. The order of bouts is also shown. The top fencers may be given "byes," and will not need to fence in the preliminary round. However, byes are usually discouraged.

TIPS FOR BEGINNERS

Warm-Up

Loosen up before fencing by doing a few stretching exercises. Get a book on exercises if you need to and follow it assiduously. They are available at most check-out counters in supermarts, drug and other stores. However, don't lift weights or do exercises that tend to shorten and tighten muscles; you need flexibility. Combine your exercises with distance running interspersed with short sprints. And practice deep breathing. I also suggest that you get a medical checkup before indulging in heavy exercise; this is a wise precaution to take not only with fencing, but before engaging in any strenuous effort after a long period of inactivity.

Instruction

I recommend that beginners take fencing lessons. However, make certain you are being taught by a qualified instructor; there are dilettantes! Of course, if you live in an area where there is no fencing instructor, you will have to rely on a book.

I believe a person can learn more from a book than many of my fellow coaches contend is possible, but it isn't easy. If you use a book, follow the instructions to the letter—and practice! Study the illustrations. Don't perpetuate your errors. These errors can become instinctive and difficult to correct. When you score touches you are especially proud of, analyze what your opponent did and how you reacted. Reconstruct situations and discuss strategy with your fellow fencers. Think! Don't become a "club champ"—a guy who can beat his or her cohorts, but is known as a "first rounder" in competition.

chapter three

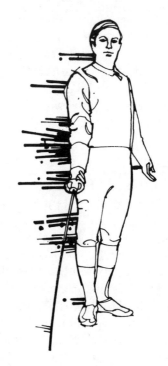

As a high school freshman, I joined a fencing club with a French fencing master, who followed a program prescribed by the French Academie D'Armes. It was demanding and strict, to say the very least. We spent several months learning footwork before we were even allowed to hold a foil!

American fencing coaches would like, but cannot afford, to follow this kind of discipline because many potentially good fencers would become restless and bored. So, you needn't worry about having to wait that long to hold a foil.

FOIL HANDLES

There are various foil handles, but I recommend the French

the weapon

handle for beginners. Only by using the French handle are you likely to develop the finger-play necessary to become a good fencer. Some fencers use other handles, (see illustration) as a crutch to compensate for poor finger-play; beginners should avoid doing this at all costs. After you have gained some experience as a competitive fencer, you may want to switch to another kind of handle, but begin with the French.

Make sure that if you're right-handed, your foil has a right-handed handle, and if you're a lefty, a left-handed handle. The wide face of the handle arches slightly, while the narrow edges curve slightly. When you hold the handle so that it arches upward from the guard to the pommel, the curve of the right-handed is to the left; the curve of the left-handed is to the right. Be certain, too, that the handle continues the line of the blade.

17

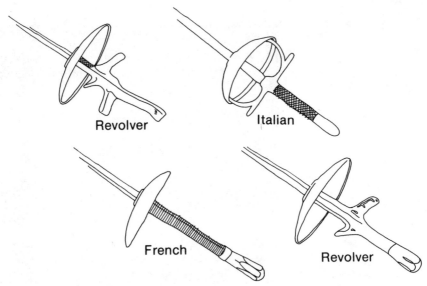

Revolver

Italian

French

Revolver

Figure 4. Various foil handles. Only the French handle should be used by beginners; the others may cause bad habits.

THE GRIP

There is only one proper way to grip the French handle. With the handle in the proper position—arching upward and curving to the left for righties, to the right for lefties—place the thumb on top of the wide side of the handle. Place the index finger in such a way that the second phalanx (the section between the fingertip and knuckle) rests against the underside of the wide face. Wrap the other three fingers around the handle so that the first phalanx of each of these fingers rests lightly on the left, narrow edge of the handle (the right edge for lefties).

Make sure that the thumb and index finger are far up on the handle, close to the pad, just inside the guard. Do not pinch or nip the handle. When properly gripped, the pommel is close to, but not quite resting on, the wrist.

When gripping the handle with the thumb on top, the fingers on the side and the hand turned slightly, the foil is in half-supination.

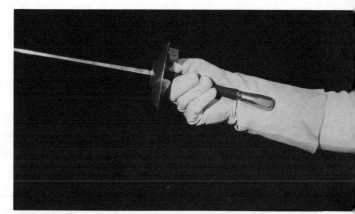

The proper grip in
half supination

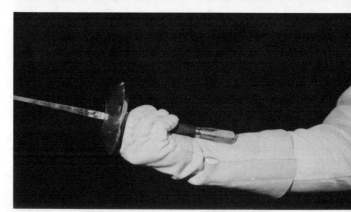

The grip in full
supination

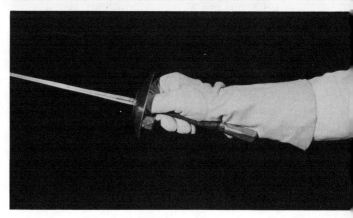

The grip in full
pronation

This is the grip you will use. There are two other positions (see illustrations): supination (the fingernails on top), and pronation (knuckles on top). For now, however, we will not be concerned with any grip except where the hand is in half-supination.

The thumb and index finger, in the main, not the wrist, control the blade. They are called manipulators. These two digits control all blade movements, whether lateral, circular, or semicircular. The other three fingers are called aids. They give assistance to the manipulators by opening and closing on the handle.

BALANCE

The tang is the short end of the blade under the guard. It is round and threaded at its end. The handle slips over the nonthreaded part and the pommel screws into the threaded tip. The tang has a different temper than the blade, and is square rather than round for part of its length.

It is very important that the tang be properly canted (tilted or slanted). If the tang is not properly canted, the weapon will feel unbalanced and your fingerplay will be impaired. If not properly mounted, the point will not be straight to the target.

When you have to replace the blade, you'll be confronted with this problem of balance. To properly balance the weapon, you'll need a vise to hold the blade and a hammer to tap the tang into the desired cant. You'll probably have to test the weapon a few times by making some lateral and circular movements with the foil before you get the right feel.

If you order a handle other than the French, your supplier will have to shorten the tang and re-thread it to obtain a good, tight fit. It is a good idea to order replacement blades precut to fit your original handle order. Otherwise, when you have to replace a blade, you'll have to cut and re-thread the blade yourself. (The die for threading is inexpensive and available in any hardware store.)

THE BLADE

The blade is rectangular in cross-section and quite flexible. Its specifications—which refer to the length of the blade, length of the

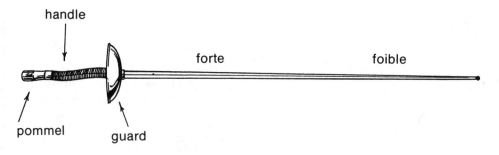

handle

forte foible

pommel guard

Figure 5. The parts of the foil

whole weapon, degree of flexibility, size of the guard, buttons or points, and the total weight—are quite specific and are set out completely in the rule book (see appendix A).

When you order blades from a supplier, upon receipt, examine every one and test for flexibility. Blades are handmade, so no two are exactly identical. Occasionally, a blade is too flexible, too stiff, or marred by carbon spots, indicating an early break. Return all flawed blades immediately. It is a good idea to have two or three replacement blades on hand at all times. There is occasional breakage, especially by beginners. However, should you have an excessive breakage of blades, you are probably fencing too close to your opponent.

Your supplier furnishes blades fitted with the same button specified for electric foils now being increasingly used in competitions. These foils are said to be closer to the weight of electric foils, and their use for practice is said to make the transition to the electric foil easier. Therefore, the small extra cost may be justified.

The material and instructions in this book are written for the right-handed fencer. To attempt a volume aimed at both right- and left-handed fencers would be confusing and a needless effort. My left-handed students throughout the years have had no problems in reversing the situations presented. References to electric foil have been made from time to time where deemed necessary. A separate section on the electric foil in Chapter Twelve treats this weapon in detail.

chapter four

Before a sprinter explodes from the starting blocks or a diver springs off a platform, they must assume the correct stances. Otherwise what follows is not likely to be successful. In fencing, the stance and the on-guard position are even more important because the fencer must continually return to the on-guard position during the course of action. It is from the on-guard position that all movements and actions emanate.

THE STANCE

Taking the correct stance, which refers to placement of the feet, is the first step in assuming the on-guard position. Place the feet at right angles and about eighteen inches apart, though the exact distance will vary among individuals. Keep your lead foot and lead

basic positions

knee pointed toward your imaginary opponent; your weight should be evenly balanced on both feet.

Note that when viewed from the front (see illustration), the lead foot hides the heel of the rear foot. This imaginary line between the lead foot and the rear heel, called the fencing line, should be maintained for all movements. It is especially important to maintain when advancing or retreating from your opponent, and at the conclusion of the lunge. Otherwise your balance will be poor and you will probably miss your opponent.

ON-GUARD POSITION

Taking the On-Guard Position

The illustration shows the ideal classical stance and on-guard

don't, you may need to make some adjustment from the ideal position. Good instructors do not insist on an identical stance for every student.

If you think an adjustment is necessary, try slightly lengthening or shortening the distance between your feet, or slightly shifting your weight from one foot to the other, or narrowing the ninety-degree angle of your feet by turning the toes of the rear foot slightly toward your opponent. However, in the last case, do not move the rear heel and be sure the lead foot always points toward the opponent; in other words, the fencing line between your lead foot and the rear heel should always be maintained.

Don't rush into any of the above adjustments. First, make certain that you have followed all of the original instructions. Departures from the ideal position are more valid when fencing with electric scoring devices; this will be discussed later.

THE TARGET AREA

The foil is the most restricted of all weapons. It is the same for men and women. It covers the trunk of the body only, excluding the

Figure 6. The foil target area

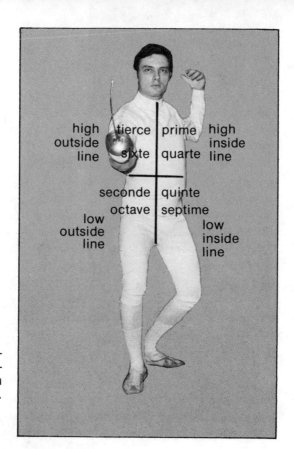

high outside line · tierce · prime · high inside line

sixte · quarte

seconde · quinte

octave · septime

low outside line · low inside line

The foil target quartered. The lines divide one area from another.

head and the limbs. The surface covered is that between the top of the collar and the lines of the groin in front, and the back and sides, down to a horizontal line across the top of the hip bones. At the shoulder, it reaches the seam of the sleeve which should pass over the humerus bone. The bib of the mask is off-target; however, its length is regulated.

Only those hits that land on-target are scored. However, there are two exceptions. These exceptions are founded on logic and you will readily understand them as you fence and encounter the situations where they are applied. First, if a fencer covers or protects the valid surface (target) with his unarmed hand or arm, the hit against his unarmed hand or arm will be scored. Second, if a fencer ducks to the floor displacing an otherwise valid area with his mask, the hit against his mask will likewise be scored.

The target area is quartered (see illustration), and eight positions are named, two in each quadrant. These positions have

On guard position in quarte

On guard position in
octave

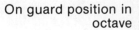

been handed down through the centuries and the terminology is still used in every country where fencing is practiced. Our main concerns are the positions of sixte, quarte, octave, and septime. The others have been obsolete for some time, although with the progress of electric fencing, made possible in part by mechanical and electrical improvements, the positions of quinte and prime have been revived to a considerable extent. This revival has been accompanied by the increasing use of angular attacks. Traditionally, in the four positions of sixte, quarte, octave, and septime, the hand is held in a supinated position; in the other four, with the

28

On guard position in
septime

hand in pronation. On-guard positions and parries bear these
named positions.

We also indicate outside and inside lines on the quartered target.
The outside lines are on the sword-arm side and the inside lines on
the other side; each is bounded by the vertical line. Above the
horizontal are the high lines; and below, the low lines. Thus we
have outside high and outside low lines and inside high and inside
low lines.

At this point in time in the evolution of the sport of fencing, we
cannot consider the positions, planes, or lines of the target as being

Figure 7. The realistic foil target

merely points of reference for instruction, though they were thought of that way for centuries. Here we must depart from the classical approach and take a much more realistic and logical position.

In our illustration, the target area is presented four-square to the viewer. However, when a fencer assumes the on-guard position, the target presented is much narrower, and some areas on it are practically inaccessible to the attacker or, equally important, obscured from the jury's view. The high and low inside lines, for instance, no longer have the same validity to an attacker; they have been placed almost out of reach. The outside low line, on the other hand, is obscured more often than not, to the jury; countless fencers have been deprived of hits to this area, simply because they were not seen.

Our conclusion must be, therefore, that the divisions of the target, as made in the past, were theoretical, determined arbitrarily and with scant attention to the frequency of hits as related to various parts of the target. The beginning fencer was led astray, both by text and personal instruction, into believing that there was equal opportunity of scoring a hit—whatever the target area. This is unrealistic. And I hope that beginners will start their training with greater awareness of the "realistic" target, as a result of this discussion.

THE FENCING MEASURE

The measure, according to classical definition, refers to the distance that separates fencers from each other, i.e., that distance from which a fencer can score a hit with a full lunge. Two fencers of different heights have different fencing measures. Instruction in fencing measure revolves around positioning the student, by foot movements, to retain his or her own distance while destroying the opponent's measure. Constant practice sharpens the ability to gauge distance to the point where it becomes a conditioned reflex.

A short fencer opposing a much taller opponent may employ a move called "the gain" to offset the disadvantage of height. From an on-guard position, the short fencer brings his rear foot forward until the rear heel touches the front heel, stealthily, and lunges from that position thereby gaining enough ground to score a successful hit against his taller adversary, all other things being equal. Unfortunately, all other conditions are not always equal. Advanced fencers usually develop excellent peripheral vision, which allows them to perceive their shorter opponent's move and step out of distance, thus retaining the advantage of their height.

chapter five

There are several movements that every fencer must master in order to master the sport as a whole.

THE ADVANCE AND THE RETREAT

The advance and the retreat are foot movements—stepping forward, or backward—from an on-guard position. They are used to maintain or gain distance on an opponent. In executing these movements, the fencer should keep the fencing line, and not move obliquely. Should this be difficult, change your stance by bringing the left toe and left knee slightly forward, toward your opponent. You may also turn both hips slightly to the right (the outside line). It is imperative, however, that you maintain the fencing line.

It is also necessary to keep the trunk of the body erect during ad-

basic movements

vance and retreat. The trunk should have no independent movement. Nor should you bob up and down; one must retain the same center of gravity as established by your own on-guard position.

To execute the advance, carry the leading foot forward about a foot's length. In stepping out, the toes are lifted first; the heel lands first and then the toes. The rear foot follows immediately. The movement is always forward with the feet just skimming the floor. Avoid the beginner's sometime habit of lifting the feet before making the forward movements.

All fencing moves must be rhythmic. The advance described is a two-count (tempo) movement. However, the advance may also be done in one count by bringing the rear foot up in such a way so that it lands on the floor *at the same time* as the front toes. Your first attempt at this one-count advance will very likely produce a

Figure 8. The advance in two tempos

Figure 9. The advance in one tempo

34

Figure 10. The retreat

thumping sound as toes and foot land together. This is caused by an exaggerated lifting of the front toes. With practice, you will soon lose the thump and the exaggeration.

It will help your skills as a fencer to vary both rhythm and the tempo. Also, you may find that the one-tempo advance followed by the lunge is faster. These separate moves can be executed with sufficient speed to make the combination in one tempo so that an opponent will be unable to steal time on you. And it may break up his or her planned tactics.

To execute the retreat from on-guard, carry the back foot to the rear and immediately follow with the front foot, skimming the floor. Maintain the same distance from your opponent in the retreat as in the advance.

The basic footwork described thus far has many variations depending upon the bout situation. The moves may be exploratory as a preparation to change the rhythm and tempo, to defend, to destroy an opponent's fencing distance, or to retain your own. All of these, and more, are determined by your level of competency

35

and tactical game, and the basic thinking of your opponent, who may be constantly moving forward or backward.

THE LUNGE

The lunge, which is the means by which an attack is delivered, has been described by many fencing masters as the most important single move. The lunge has two parts. The first is the development, which is an extension of the sword arm combined with foot and leg actions that enables the attacker to reach and hit his opponent. The second is the return or recovery to guard, which puts the attacker out of reach of a riposte and from which he can initiate another action.

You should think of the lunge—or the development and the return to guard—as one unbroken movement and remember that it has not been fully executed until the return to guard has been completed. Over the years, I have noticed an almost uniform tendency on the part of beginners, and some mature fencers, to hang out there awhile before recovering to guard. For now, you are advised to return as swiftly as possible. If you do stay out there, fully extended, it should be with the intention or hope that your opponent will "take" the blade, from which you will escape by a disengage (which should be made with the arm still extended) and impale your impetuous opponent. You should practice this move with a cooperative partner, repeatedly and alternatively, from sixte and quarte. This is also a very good exercise in learning how and when to disengage from pressure on your blade.

Although we should think of the lunge as one flowing, unbroken movement, for purposes of discussion, we will refer to the development and the recovery.

Development

First, in the sequence of the lunge is the arm extension. The extended arm always precedes the foot movement. Otherwise, you will be telegraphing your punch and opening yourself to an action by your opponent. If of any competence, he or she will steal time

basic movements

The arm extension
as seen from the
front and from the
side

The lunge as seen
from the front

on you. The importance of a proper and correctly executed arm extension cannot be overemphasized. It identifies and establishes the right of way, directs the point to the target, and aids in deception as to your intentions to attack. Your blade must continuously threaten the opponent's valid surface.

The arm extension should be swift but smooth, as though you were lengthening your arm. The action takes place at the elbow; there should be no punching from the shoulder.

Second in the sequence of the lunge are the foot and leg movements that deliver the point and make the hit. Raise the toes of the forward foot, thrust forward with the heel just clear of the floor, and simultaneously straighten and extend the left leg, landing on the front foot, *heel first*, with the sole of the foot following. The rear leg reaches its full extension just before the foot hits the floor. The illustration demonstrates the correct conclusion of the movement with the lower leg perpendicular, the upper leg almost horizontal, and the left leg fully extended with the trunk also

Two phases of the lunge, the arm and leg movements at the beginning of the lunge, and the completion of the lunge for a hit.

perpendicular. The left foot remains on the floor. With the intensity of the lunge, this foot may move forward but must not leave the floor. The fencer must also take care that the foot does not roll over to its inside edge.

The trailing arm is also important in the lunge. It is thrown *straight back briskly* to a point just above and parallel to the leg, with palm to the inside, as shown in the illustration. The arm is thrown back simultaneously with the arm and leg extension. This may be compared to the law of motion which states that for every action there is an equal and opposite reaction.

This arm action assists in the speed of the lunge and the retention of balance, and also in keeping the fencing line. Should you twist your hand in the throw-back motion, you may distort the position of the trunk, lose balance, and most likely throw your blade point off-target.

There are two imperatives in proper execution of the lunge. *Don't* roll the rear foot over onto the inside edge of the sole. (See illustration.) Don't let your trunk lean over the leading leg; keep the same relative center of gravity as in the on-guard position. Should either of these rules be violated, your recovery from the lunge will be seriously affected.

These are crucial points and should be closely observed in practice sessions throughout your whole fencing career. Any errors of omission or commission will develop into conditioned reflexes that may be impossible to correct later.

You should strive for perfection in the execution of these foot and leg movements; they are constants; they constitute the complete foundation for fencers in the international class, proven in world competitions.

Recovery

To return to on-guard, first the toes of the front foot are lifted simultaneously with a pushing back of the heel, forcing the body back. The rear leg is flexed and *with* the knee, pulls the body backward. The knee points toward the toes of the rear foot—ending over the foot. There is no independent movement of the body.

Fencer on left demonstrates the error of rolling the back foot onto the inside edge of the sole.

The front toe and heel leave the floor *last* and almost duplicate their position when on the lunge. The front foot is lowered toward the floor and planted on the floor as it is going backward. It should not be planted from an unnatural height.

From the lunge, you may also recover *forward* to guard. The feet, however, should be brought up closer together than in the original on-guard position; from here you may initiate another action.

Variations on the Lunge

The Jump Advance (Balestra). Almost self-explanatory, the jump advance is executed from the on-guard position. The right leg is extended from the knee and the foot is pressed down and slightly

41

backward (not forward as in the lunge); body weight is then shifted forward, *bouncing* away from the left ankle and landing simultaneously on the floor with both soles. The arm is extended with the jump (the trunk remains in its more or less static position). The extension and the jump are followed immediately by a lunge. This advance may be viewed as a preparation to attack; it is fast, done in one tempo, and should gain some distance.

The Jump Backward. This, too, is almost self-explanatory—the jump backward is executed from an on-guard position. The left leg is extended back with some extra impetus, the right leg is then slung backward with the jump. You should land with both feet simultaneously in an on-guard position. Should you have difficulty with the jump backward, start by straightening and swinging the left leg backward, aided by a push from the front leg, again landing on both feet simultaneously.

THE FLÈCHE

The flèche is a running attack and depends on many factors, but mostly surprise, for its success. Failure to hit submits the fencer to considerable peril from a shot to the back after passing. The photographs demonstrate this action and premise very well. I have never allowed my foil fencers to flèche in a competitive situation until they had achieved perfect execution in practice—and then only sparingly. Traditionally, the flèche is carried out by executing an arm extension, then inclining the trunk forward almost to the point of losing balance. Then, the left foot is carried forward and over the leading leg. This first step and the hit occur simultaneously, the next steps take the fencer past the opponent on his quarte side. The rules prohibit collisions; should a collision occur, the flèche has been improperly executed.

The flèche has more validity when a small step is taken with the right foot and the body weight shifted to the right leg which is bent slightly. The fencer then pushes off or springs from this leg. The left leg is then brought to the front and over the front leg and the fencer continues past the opponent.

To execute the flèche, the fencer on the right, from absence of blade, extends his arm leaning into his right knee with lifting of back foot (top). He makes the hit as he crosses with his left leg (center), and passes on quarte side after the hit (bottom).

Arm extension exercises — the beginning position (left) and the end position (right)

You may use a combination—a step across, a lunge, and flèche. In this case, the body is not inclined forward. The first movement is the stride across with the left leg to the front; the body takes part in the leg movement, rather than preceding the leg movement as in the traditional flèche. This combination makes it possible to execute a second intention attack (discussed in Chapter Ten) that is impossible with traditional execution of the flèche.

ARM EXTENSION EXERCISES

Exercises will help you to acquire a proper and smooth arm extension. Perform them from the proper stance and on-guard position but standing erect until extension is smooth and easy. Raise your elbow to about shoulder height and then direct the blade and forearm to your left to form a right *angle* with the blade parallel to the floor. Then bring your blade and forearm back into line with the point directed immediately toward an imaginary opponent. Do this repeatedly from this same position. Then, from a smaller angle with the blade pointed obliquely to the left, bring the blade into line again. Next, from an imaginary engagement with the angle, of course, being much less, bring the blade into line again.

This exercise should be performed slowly. You will notice that there is no punching from the shoulder; that your arm extension is from the elbow.

In variation of this exercise, the fencer, from an on-guard position using the elbow only, directs the point toward the ceiling, as in a salute. Then, using the elbow only, he brings his blade down and into line again. There should be no forward motion of the shoulder. These exercises should be a part of every practice session.

When you have learned to execute a proper arm extension, go through the exercises again but, from full on-guard position, rather than standing erect. In each case, *after* your point is in line, *lunge*! With sufficient practice you will have learned to extend—get the right of way—and with the foot always following the extension, you will have acquired a fast disengage at the same time and a good straight thrust.

chapter six

The following terms are used to describe the most important blade positions and movements in fencing.

BASIC BLADE POSITIONS

There are three basic positions in which a fencer can hold his or her blade: the on-guard position, discussed earlier; as an invitation (invito); and with point-in-line.

As an Invitation

When the blade is held in such a position so as to induce an opponent to attack—into the line or lines left open—it is said to be held as an invitation. The size of the invitation is usually determined by the fencer's level of proficiency. Against an unknown op-

basic blade work

ponent, the invitation would be smaller; against a known fencer, it would be larger. Against a truly experienced fencer, the invitation would be slight, but evident to the experienced eye.

With Point-in-Line

To have point-in-line is to have the arm extended and the point threatening a valid surface. Should the point *not* threaten a valid target, then it would be considered an invitation and not a point in line. According to the rules, when an attack starts against a point already in line, the attacker must first deflect his adversary's weapon. If the blade is not deflected and the attacker hits, he would not have the right of way, and if hit, he would in effect have impaled himself and the hit would be scored against him.

The fencer on the
left holds his blade
as an invitation.

The "point in line"

These fencers are on guard, their blades engaged in sixte.

Many fencers use the point-in-line as a defensive measure, done deliberately. The intention is to evade an attack on the blade (dérobement) and thus retain the right of way. Many beginners, however, use the point-in-line to ward off an attack in desperation or as a result of ineffective parries. This action or tactic can be easily recognized, and it is very probable that an experienced fencer will deflect the blade without difficulty.

THE ENGAGEMENT

When two fencers are facing each other and their blades are in contact in any guard position, they are engaged. In sixte, for example, each blade would have the opposite blade to the outside in contact with each other. Engagements usually are in sixte and quarte; however, fencers can also be engaged in octave or septime. At all times, be aware of your blade position in relation to that of your opponent.

49

When the blades are not in contact, the fencers are said to be fencing with absence of blade. Absence of blade can also be referred to as an invitation to your opponent to attack into the open target. You will find, as you progress in your fencing, that tactics and the blade position have a relationship, one factor determines the other.

Change of Engagement

To change engagement is to change the line from which the fencers are engaged to an opposite line—as from an engagement in sixte into one in quarte. A change in engagement is a simple form of "taking the blade" (see Chapter Eight) and opens up the opponent's line of defense. It is accomplished by manipulating blade position by use of the fingers, called finger play. The fencer, engaged in sixte, drops the point, passing it *under* the opponent's blade and engages it in the new line, i.e., in quarte. As the point is dropped, and passed under the other blade, the hand moves over to quarte simultaneously with the contact of the other blade.

The change of engagement can be deceived and it is therefore necessary that the finger play precede any arm movement; do not change the level of the hand. The opponent's blade must be taken as soon as possible. Should you not find your opponent's blade in making the change, you will be still able to parry, *if* your finger play precedes arm movement.

You should practice changes—those *not* involving blade contact as well as those that do—assiduously. You will discover, as you progress, various positions from which you may attack or defend. These positions will aid in preparation for attacks. In today's fencing, preparations for attack have a major place in your repertoire.

Double Change of Engagement

In making a double change of engagement, you return to the original engagement—e.g., from sixte to quarte and from quarte back to sixte. To succeed, it must be made with great speed, with small movements of the point and blade, and proper positioning of

The fencer on the right disengages and makes the hit.

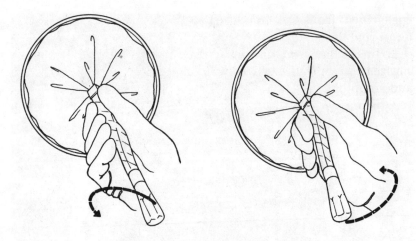

Figure 11. Details of finger play

the hand. The beginning fencer will have difficulty in making a single change of engagement let alone a double change. And it may very well be that for the beginner its greatest value is as an exercise to aid the development of good finger play.

A double change of engagement, coupled with a disengage and lunge, executed with deliberation, will also aid the precipitate fencer in properly synchronizing his or her arm extension and foot movement in making the lunge. Frequently, in this exercise, after the second change of engagement, beginners start the foot movement *before* the disengage and arm extension. This exercise clearly demonstrates that moving the foot first is slow and wrong, that the hand is quicker than the foot. Also, recall that the right of way applies to an arm extension, and not to a precipitate movement of the foot.

Finger-play Exercises

Skillful finger play is the secret to good blade work, not only in change of engagement, but in many other fencing movements as well. Below are some exercises to assist you:

1. From a stand-up, on-guard position, practice a change of

engagement from sixte to quarte, and from quarte to sixte, slowly, *using your fingers*.

2. In the same position as above, practice double changes of engagement with no pause between changes—repeatedly, but slowly and smoothly.

3. From a sitting-down position, change engagement from sixte

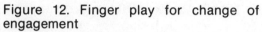

Figure 12. Finger play for change of engagement

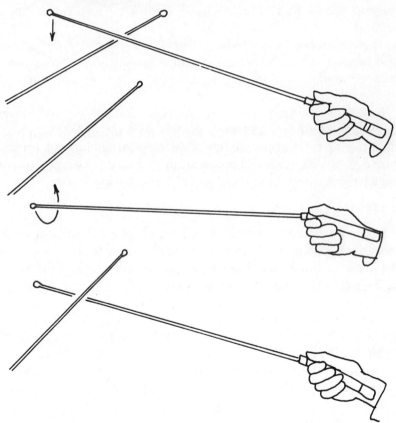

Top: The engagement in sixte. Center: The blade is lowered by the manipulators while relaxing the aids. Bottom: The opposite finger actions raise the blade to engagement in the opposite line.

to quarte, then disengage again with a full-arm extension and lunge. Repeat—but from an on-guard position in quarte.

4. From the same position, do double changes of engagement, from sixte and then from quarte. After each double change of engagement, disengage again with full-arm extension and lunge.

5. From a stand-up, on-guard position, extend your arm and with your fingers, all of them, make small circles with the point from right to left and then from left to right. Speed is not a requirement here; just the opposite is the case. One variation to the above exercise would be to take aim at a door knob and make circles around it.

These exercises have additional benefits in respect to disengaging and lunging. They should aid you to make proper arm extensions before moving your leading foot in the lunge, discouraging this precipitate movement.

6. Lunge against a wall or other target, and, as you hit, loosen the last three fingers and keep the point on-target with just your thumb and forefinger; on return to on-guard, close all fingers. Make your hits against the wall from pretended sixte and quarte engagements, and as you hit, cover the opposite lines.

THE HIT

A hit or touch is the end result of a thrust of one kind or another from some position of the hand or hand and arm. How the hit is made and acknowledged depends upon whether or not the fencer is fencing with a nonelectric or electric foil.

Electric foil refers to a system of scoring in which fencer and foil are so equipped that hits can be electrically detected. This scoring system is being used more and more in formal fencing competitions. While it does not affect basic fencing procedures, hits are scored in a slightly different way in electric foil. That is why I suggested earlier that your blades be fitted with a mock electric point. This won't affect your game but will aid in making the transition to electric scoring.

The rules applying to nonelectric foil require that "every hit must arrive clearly and distinctly to be counted as a touch." A jury makes the decision on the materiality of the touch. The rules on

The traditional method of teaching the hit to a beginner. The point is "placed" on the target with the aid of the fingers. A smooth arm extension follows so that the point arrives clearly and distinctly.

electric foil on the other hand, provide that "the pressure that must be exerted upon the point to cause the scoring machine to register must be more than 500 grams, i.e., the spring in the button must be able to push back this weight." In this case, the machine "sees" the hit and decides its materiality.

In nonelectric foil, the point is placed on target first with the fingers and fixed, then the arm is extended to the target with the fist raised slightly. The fencer pushes the hit so that the bending of the blade and the raised fist will indicate a hit to the jury, i.e., arriving clearly and distinctly. The fencer here also strives for perpendicularity of the blade and point in relation to the target as he or she makes the hit.

In electric foil, the fencer needs only to depress the point—breaking the circuit. Through practice, one gauges the amount of thrust or push necessary to do this. You are not compelled to forcefully push the point home. And here, too, the fencer is concerned with the perpendicularity of the blade, but not to the same extent. He or she has much more freedom now to explore a target with angulated thrusts, better able to "place" a point without a forceful thrust. And the fencer can, when parried, return more quickly to a defensive position; there is less chance he or she will have overextended or overpushed the point in the lunge.

chapter seven

There are three simple attacks—the straight thrust, the disengage, and the cut-over. Each involves only one movement of the blade, and each attack is executed in one period of fencing time, defined by AFLA as "being the time required to perform one simple fencing action." Success is dependent on proper timing and speed of execution. *No* deception is involved, at least no *purposeful* deception. Since all attacks are delivered by the lunge, a proper arm extension from the elbow may involve some deception because the extension might be completed before your opponent is aware of it.

THE STRAIGHT THRUST

The straight thrust is executed by simply extending the arm in a straight line and hitting the target (or missing). It should be practiced from all positions and from varying distances. Most impor-

simple attacks

tant is that you do not "punch" from the shoulder, and that your arm extension precedes any movement of the leading foot. Ideally the straight thrust is executed so that you cover your own target. For instance, if in sixte guard, move the hand left so that the hand is in quarte as you score your hit. If in quarte guard, move the hand to the right, i.e., into sixte. This move of the hand, left or right, should be made smoothly; if you move your hand jerkily, you will probably miss the target. By covering, you force in effect your opponent to make his or her own new offensive action to an anticipated open line.

THE DISENGAGE

The disengage is an indirect attack and presupposes that you and your opponent are in a state of engagement, i.e., your blades are

Figure 13. The straight thrust. From an engagement in sixte (top), the fencer on right notices that his opponent is uncovered; he extends into uncovered sixte (center) and delivers a straight thrust with lunge (bottom).

crossed and in contact with each other. It is executed by passing the point of your foil from a line of engagement into the opposite line and lunging.

Finger play is of paramount importance in this attack. When changing line, don't swing the arm from one side to the other;

Figure 14. The disengage. From an engagement in sixte (top), the fencer on right passes his point *under* opponent's blade (center) and delivers an attack by disengage with lunge (bottom).

manipulate the point. Thumb and index finger must move the point so that it passes under the opponent's blade and then is raised again in line with your target. Though the disengage usually brings the attacker's blade *under* the other blade, the disengage may be either under or over the blade. Be sure on the disengage

Figure 15. The cut-over. From an engagement in sixte (top), the fencer on right draws his blade up and over opponent's blade, clearing it. He then extends his arm into quarte and lunges (bottom).

that the foot movement does not precede the blade movement. The disengage, arm extension, and following lunge should be one flowing movement.

Here again, you should cover your own target. In essence, in covering you close the line of attack left open.

It is usually in the coach and student situation that we initiate actions from a state of engagement. In the past, foil fencing was said to be a "conversation with the blades." Now, however, fencers usually fence with absence of blade. In a student-teacher situation, the teacher will silently signal that he wants a disengage by putting pressure on the blade. His detachment of the blade from an engagement called for, and still does, a straight thrust.

THE CUT-OVER (COUPÉ)

This is a simple disengagement executed by passing *over* your opponent's blade, sliding your blade *up*, clearing the tip of your opponent's blade, extending the arm, and lunging to your target in a straight thrust movement. When sliding up, your hand should be in pronation, changing to half-supination after clearing the tip.

There is some peril in using the cut-over because in clearing your opponent's blade, your point could be off target at this time, or if you execute your move improperly, your opponent could score. A hit scored on your opponent's attack is called a stop hit.

However, the cut-over can be effective, especially when executed against an opponent's pressure on your blade or when you precede your cut-over with a slight beat and your opponent does an answer beat. It is then that you deceive with a very fast cut-over. This shot probably has a better chance for success when delivered to your opponent's back or side from an angulated arm position.

A PERIOD OF FENCING TIME

Rhythm, time and tempo are the most important concepts in fencing. Once you have mastered the basic movements, you must learn to relate them to each other in a disciplined and organized way. A period of fencing time is a basic unit in the whole organiza-

From absence of blade, fencer on left begins a cut-over. Notice that his point makes no threat.

tion of fencing. A certain amount of time is required to perform one simple action. Examples of actions which, in themselves, constitute one period of fencing time are the advance, retreat, lunge, arm extension, disengage, and so on. Under AFLA rules, an attack executed in one period of fencing time is not subject to a counterattack; it must be parried and the parry followed by a riposte, after which the original attacker can attack again. In general, this rule prevents the fencer on defense from taking the attack as long as the fencer on offense executes his attacks in one period of fencing time. An opportunity to reverse the situation comes, however, when an opponent uses an attack executed in more than one period of fencing time. These attacks, called compound attacks, are subject to counterattack. It is at this point that a fencer's sensitivity to time and tempo becomes very important. A counteraction, to be successful and valid against a compound attack, must precede the final movement of the compound attack by one period of fencing time. Whether or not the counterattack has been made in time is decided by the director. The touch is awarded, or not, according to his judgment. These calls of the director cannot be the subject of an appeal should either the attacker or defender believe that he had the time.

To demonstrate an attacking action, whether simple or compound, the instructor frequently breaks the action or actions into separate parts. For example, in the disengage, the student drops the point under the blade (count one), then extends the arm (count two), and then lunges (count three), thus stretching one fencing movement to occupy three periods of fencing time. In this case, a counteraction by a defender would be successful if it preceded the final movement. This exercise helps the beginner to understand both the new movement and a period of fencing time.

As the novice becomes more experienced, he or she will learn that the process also works in the other direction—compound attacks can be delivered in one period of fencing time, if the foot and blade actions are executed simultaneously. A progressive compound attack—by disengage-disengage, by beat and advance, or by another combination of movements—can be made in one period of fencing time, and it is practically impossible for an opponent to gain time against it. However, a fairly high level of competency is required. If the attacker pauses on his disengage feint, or withdraws his arm, or breaks up his compound attack, the counteraction would have the right of way, and if executed in such time as to precede the final movement of the attack, it would be given the touch.

chapter eight

Preparations for attack are those movements which precede or prepare the way for offensive actions. They may consist of (1) attacks on the opponent's blade; (2) foot movements, a step or series of steps which may be forward or backward; or, (3) blade actions that take possession of an opponent's blade while maintaining contact with it.

ATTACKS ON THE BLADE

The Beat and Change-beat

A sharp blow upon your opponent's blade made in order to deflect and open the line to a thrust or a feint is called a beat. When made from a mere contact or an engagement, the blade is detached

preparations for attack

momentarily and then brought back crisply to its deflecting action. Traditionally, the beat and change-beat (described below) opposed the forte against the foible. But with longer distances separating present-day fencers, the blades usually make contact at the same height. Therefore, beats are now made with the foible, but are of an exploratory nature. A beat is also made occasionally to draw a reaction (a bringing of the blade back to position), which may be deceived by a disengage.

In making the beat, avoid continuing the deflecting action to a point beyond being able to make a thrust straight forward. Refrain from repetitious use of the beat. All elements of surprise will be lost.

In the change-beat, the beat is executed in a line opposite to the engagement. Finger play is more involved than in the beat. Beats

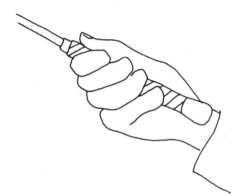

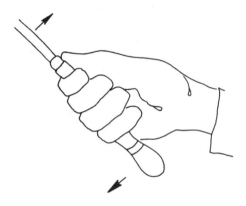

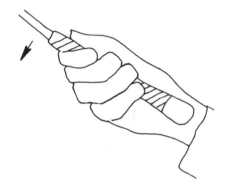

Figure 16. To use finger play in the execution of a beat, from the hand position of half supination (left), a fencer "opens aids" (manipulates thumb and forefinger) from opposite blade (right), and then "closes aids," (bottom) bringing the foil's handle back to his wrist and causing the opposite blade to be struck crisply.

or change-beats, in combination with, and to introduce a lunge or jump lunge, appear to be the ingredients for a successful attack, containing to a marked degree all the elements of surprise. Beats may also be used to deflect a point in line; caution is indicated in this situation, however, as the beats may be expected and therefore easily deceived.

The Graze (Froissement)

A thrust made diagonally and down, strongly, to sharply deflect the opponent's blade to the side is known as the graze. Made from an engagement, the arm is extended slightly, the wrist is flexed, and the hand brought into pronation. The forte of the blade is opposed to the foible. Most fencers use the graze sparingly, and then perhaps only against the fencer with poor control of his blade, or whose grip appears to be insecure.

The Pressure

A fencer sometimes applies a subtle possessive pressure with more continuous contact to create a reaction. This reaction is more likely to be produced if the pressure comes immediately after a change of engagement. This introduces a surprise element and could pave the way to a disengage or a one-two.

The Glide

The glide is a forward movement of the blade with continuous contact, sliding toward the target left open by an uncovered guard position. I suggest that it be used against a poor sixte or quarte guard. When your opponent becomes conscious of the oncoming point, he will probably cover in a wide outside target position. The pressure exerted by his blade is the signal for your disengage. There is little to distinguish the glide from the straight thrust, except this continuous sliding contact. Your opponent's response in deflecting creates the opportunity for the disengage.

THE ADVANCE AND RETREAT

The movements of the feet in stepping forward or backward were the traditional means of maintaining distance. Today, they are used extensively as preparations for attack, usually in combination with another preparation. Foot movements and blade movements in combination can be employed very effectively in securing touches.

TAKINGS OF THE BLADE (Prises de Fer)

Blade actions that take possession of an opponent's blade while maintaining contact with it have their own separate movements and beginning and end positions, if properly executed and appropriate to the bout situation. (Some authorities classify these blade actions as attacks on the blade.) Recall that in discussing the target area we illustrated and discussed the *outside lines*, high and low, and the *inside lines*, high and low. Keep these lines in mind as you read and as you execute the takings of the blade in practice. It will be helpful.

Binds

Binds are blade actions that carry an opponent's blade from a high line to an *opposite* low line; or, from a low line to an *opposite* high line. One condition must prevail: Binds must be executed only against a *fully extended arm*. In bouts, you may find that binds from low to high lines have little chance to succeed in scoring a hit, but, practice all the binds anyway, because they will give you increasing "feel" for the blade, an indispensable skill in a complete fencer.

To execute a bind from high line to opposite low line, move your blade, with a bent arm, laterally; take possession of the oncoming and threatening blade, then pivot over the blade and carry it diagonally, point first, to the opposite low line. From sixte, moving laterally first, the pivot takes the blade to septime. From quarte, moving first laterally, the pivot takes the blade to octave. As you finish the diagonal and hit, a simultaneous raising of the hand will prevent your opponent from escaping your bind. In practice, however, don't raise the hand. Allow a cooperative partner to escape. In practice, alternate roles with your partner in order that both of you learn as much about binds as possible.

To execute a bind from the outside low line (octave) to the opposite high lines, make the octave parry, take possession, forte to foible, immediately and gather and raise the blade to carry it across to the opposite high line. To take the blade directed to your septime (inside low), again take possession, forte to foible, with the septime parry and carry the blade across to the opposite high line.

In present-day fencing, attempts to take the blade will usually be met with a counteraction. An analysis of the binds will lead you to

Figure 17. To execute the bind from high to opposite low line against an extended arm, fencer on right parries quarte (top) and, maintaining contact of the blades, pivots *over* opposing blade, "taking" it down (center), and makes his thrust into septime (bottom).

the discovery that the binds can be easily parried. Therefore, your execution of the binds must be technically perfect if they are to succeed at all.

However, an opportunity may arise to take an opponent's blade and score. This will be dependent upon the levels to which you have conditioned your technique and reflexive (motor) skills. This score may spell victory, and there is infinite satisfaction in being able to take advantage of an opponent's momentary lapse.

All of these binds should be considered as preparations; the action that follows each bind should be the straight thrust that hits. This thrust may be executed as a feint and a disengage, made from your opponent's parry, executed by his return to guard.

The Croisé (The Cross)

The taking of the blade in the croisé is from the high line to the low line, but the blade is not brought across diagonally. It is carried to the low line on the same line as the engagement. To execute the croisé, take the attacker's blade by opposing your forte to his foible and then bear down on his blade, *lowering* your wrist and forearm. When the opponent's blade is taken from sixte, the hand and wrist should be in full supination; when the opponent's blade is taken from quarte, the hand and wrist should be in pronation. The blade in both cases is angulated toward the flank. With completion, the arm is fully extended and followed by the lunge.

The Envelopment

The envelopment is a blade action by which you take an opponent's blade with the contact opposing *forte to foible* and with a clockwise rotation of the wrist, describe a limited circle that returns both blades to the original line. The contact is maintained throughout. The envelopment should be executed only from sixte against a fully extended arm. Just before the enveloping blade has completed its circle, the arm is extended and the offensive action is initiated.

Figure 18. From an engagement in sixte (top), the fencer on right rotates his wrist in a clockwise circular movement (center) that returns blades to the original line of engagement. He then extends his arm and delivers a straight thrust by a lunge (bottom).

The hit — after taking from octave to opposite high line

Analyzing "Taking" Blade Actions

When you have acquired some proficiency in the execution of these "taking" blade actions, you should study them further, even if only vicariously in an easy chair at home. The long contact of the blades as they glide in a rail-like path with increasing pressure, opens up many interesting possibilities. Having completed the preparations, what form should the attack take? What parries can be taken? Should a disengage be made off the pressure? When? What footwork if any is used? What part does distance play? What kind of counteraction may be taken? What are the differences in binds taken from one engagement as against another engagement? This kind of analysis applied to fencing actions in general will help your tactical game keep pace with the physical forms performed in practice. You will find it rewarding to discuss fencing actions with advanced competitors at fencing meets. Most take satisfaction in passing on their knowledge. (You might find an amateur coach for your club or group.) Also, you can ask the director to tell you where you went wrong, respectfully.

Defenses Against Takings of the Blade

First, an analysis of takings of the blade will lead you to the discovery that they can be easily parried. Second, from a bind taken in sixte with the thrust directed to octave, return to guard in septime. From a bind taken in quarte with the thrust directed to septime, return to guard in octave. From a bind taken from octave to sixte, return to guard in quarte. And, from a bind taken from septime, return to guard in sixte. From an envelopment, return to guard in sixte.

The return to guard is taken with opposition, but not prematurely. Permit the attacker to get into the final part of his thrust before giving way to the withdrawal and bending of your arm. A disengage, properly timed, will impale the attacker.

chapter nine

I believe it was Napoleon who said, "The whole art of war consists in a well thought-out defense, together with a swift and bold offensive . . . one must lead his opponent to give battle under the most unfavorable conditions."

These words from a master of war have some simple application to the fencer—he is taught to hit and not be hit himself. One has this dual problem of how to *attack* with success and how to *defend* with success. And, how to create favorable situations for the scoring of touches.

If we were able to find two fencers of equal competency in every respect, an impossible task, it is almost certain that in their bout, the attacker would be the victor. On the one hand, the attacker would be distinguished by almost indefinable factors deeply hidden within his mental and nervous system that provide a men-

defense

tal edge. Also, the defender is always behind the attacker in time. He must guess, he must deduce, the intentions of the attacker and perhaps be required to put together a combination of actions to thwart the attack. Therefore, the defender is under considerably more nervous strain than the attacker and his or her energy is exhausted much sooner. As a result of these facts, the defender is much more likely to defend with instinctive defensive actions at some point in the bout, and these are easily deceived.

These untaught, instinctively performed actions can be avoided, if not altogether, then in a very large part. It is part of the fencer's training to substitute reasoned, effective, defensive moves for instinctive and less effective ones.

To do this, the complete fencer must form the defensive game by intensive, repetitive practice so as to acquire perfection in execution of every possible defensive move in all the categories. Practice with a cooperative partner, varying tempos and rhythms. Also fence with as many uncooperative fencers as possible. It is one means to the desired end.

One must know and understand the meaning of every counterattack and every manner and means of opposing preparations for attack from your opponent. In this way, you will be better able to combat the greater nervous strain common to the defender. Through these means, you will learn an intelligent choice of reflexive actions suitable for every opportunity. Your defensive actions executed to frustrate an opponent, are a tactic that often leads to victory. Ultimately, you will be able, by conditioned reflexes, to preselect the best of several actions.

CATEGORIES OF DEFENSE

There are four categories of defense—parries, foot and leg actions, displacements of the body, counterattacks and attacks on the preparations. The parries are blade actions which deflect; the good (effective) parry confers upon the defender the right of way and the right to a riposte. The foot and leg actions are movements made to keep one's distance and thus avoid being hit; they may be thought of as maneuvers to place the attacker at a disadvantage. Displacements of the body are movements such as ducking and side-stepping. Keep in mind the rule about displacement of a valid target with an invalid surface and the possibility of a touch being scored against you when you use them.

Though counterattacks and attacks on preparation will be dealt with in separate chapters, I am grouping them together here because I believe that defense is something more than the execution of parries. I prefer to regard the whole subject of defense as a system that is conceptual in nature—and not as something fragmented. And, if a fencing action has as one of its purposes the avoidance of being touched, then its description, its use, belong under the heading of "defense."

Counterattacks are defined in the rule book as "offensive or defensive-offensive actions executed during the opponent's attack." Attacks on the preparation, founded on surprise, are movements executed before an opponent's attack has begun.

Before we go on to the first category of defense, I would like to caution fencers that many directors will refer to all defensive actions as counteractions, rather than describing them as they appear in the official rules. You may be given a touch or be deprived of a touch on the basis of this disparity between your ideas and the director's. In this case, you have a right to have your action properly described by the director. If the decision is still adverse, you will have to comply with his ideas, or "fence for the director."

The same is the case when you believe your stop hit is in time but it is not allowed—on the basis of the statement that the attack was continuous. It may be that this director rarely or never permits a stop hit. You will lose any appeal here because it most certainly will be decided as a judgment call—the stop was not in time. Here again, fence for the director; forget your stop hits! Caution!! These are human judgments; accept them with good grace.

There are many good directors, however, who will observe the fencing phrase and require an attack to be "correctly executed," allowing an immediate riposte after an effective parry, or after a finding of the blade on a feint, and allowing a stop that precedes the conclusion of an attack by a period of fencing time. In these cases, you may exhaust and use every defensive action in your repertoire.

PARRIES

As we said, parries are those blade actions which deflect the opponent's blade and point (at least momentarily) and are effective enough to clear your own target area.

Lateral Parries

When a fencer moves his blade and hand across his body laterally, thus deflecting his opponent's blade, he is making a lateral parry. Two of the lateral parries, those of sixte and quarte, are also referred to as simple, direct, or instinctive parries. In your mind's

From on guard in a good covered sixte (left), the *beginning* position for the quarte parry, the fencer moves his hand and blade so that he is in a good covered quarte, the *end* position for the parry, which is also the beginning position for the sixte parry (right).

eye, bring forth an image of a caveman with a club knocking or deflecting another club directed to these areas. He would *very roughly* make similar protective moves with his club. I have used this example countless times to illustrate that these are instinctive moves—and to demonstrate the ease with which they may be deceived.

In the quarte parry, a fencer in the guard position of sixte moves his hand and blade so that he is in a quarte guard. When he reverses this move exactly—from quarte to the end position of sixte —he has performed another lateral parry, the parry of sixte. In executing these two parries, notice that the hand is held at breast height, both at the beginning and at the conclusion of the parry. Also, the lateral movement must go sufficiently far across to protect or "cover" that target area with the entire blade. Don't change the height of the hand, i.e., don't sugar any strawberries!

Equally important is not to move your hand and blade too far—don't parry for your next-door neighbor. Let the parry be sufficient—that's all. And move the hand and blade across in one piece. Don't let the point drag behind the hand; don't let the point precede the hand. If you do either, you won't be making an effective parry.

I recommend that the hand be held in half-supination throughout the lateral moves. Some fencers rotate the hand into a pronated position, thumb on top, in making the quarte parry. There is good argument to support either view.

In both these parries, carry the point at a height that is approximately under your opponent's nose. This will vary slightly with each individual. In practice, lower the point in going across to differing levels. When you get to where the blade is parallel to the floor, you will have no steel with which to deflect an on-coming blade. This exercise will enable you soon to discover at which level the point should be carried across.

Circular Parries

Circular parries, also known as counterparries or counter, may be thought of as invented parries. There is no doubt in my mind that the "circles of iron" described by Rafael Sabatini in one of his exciting novels of swords and swordsmen are circular parries.

The circular or counterparry is executed by describing an elliptical-circular movement with the blade. The point passes under the opponent's blade and returns to its initial position. This counter is made from either sixte or quarte position. The counter-sixte has been described as a clockwise movement and the counterquarte as a counterclockwise movement. Oppose the part of your blade nearest the guard (the forte) to that part of your opponent's blade nearest the point (the foible).

These counters are performed by finger play and *not* by a circular movement of the hand or forearm. When you make them, be certain that, on completion, the point returns to its original twelve-o'-clock position. Otherwise, you may not deflect the blade, but instead direct the opponent's point to your own target.

Circular or counterparries are also made to deflect attacks to the low lines, i.e., to octave or septime. In these parries, the point

The end position for the octave parry (left); the blade point has described a half-circle counterclockwise from 12 o'clock high. The defending blade must sufficiently deflect to the outside so that its point does not touch the opponent off-target. Otherwise, you will deprive yourself of a riposte. The end position for the septime parry (right). A half-circle was described by the blade point from 12 o'clock high, but clockwise.

starts at six o'clock and, passing *over* the opponent's blade, returns to that position. The finger play is assisted by some slight wrist action—but again there is no change of hand level.

Half-circle, Low-line Parries

Half-circle, low-line parries are referred to by some fencers as vertical parries, and are used to deflect attacks to the low lines and to deflect a blade from a low-line engagement to a high line. These parries are made by describing a half-circle. From sixte, they deflect the on-coming blade to the *outside low line* (octave parry); from quarte, they deflect to the *inside low line* (septime parry). Make certain that your point is to the outside and not in line with your opponent's off-target area; otherwise you will be deprived of a riposte.

Rules for Parrying

Some very important considerations are applicable to all parries. Although your blade can make contact with your opponent's blade at many points, in a successful and effective parry, the strong part of your blade (the forte) is opposed to and contacts the weak part of the oncoming blade (the foible). (One exception is the beat parry, in which the beat is made by the foible alone, with no lateral movement of the hand.) Also, in the high lateral parries of sixte and quarte, your point and hand must be high enough to exert sufficient leverage to deflect, and for the low parries, only a displacement of the blade is required—the hand does not change from its breast-high position.

Your parries will usually be most effective when combined with a retreat to keep the distance. However, occasionally, a short advance to close the distance, opportunely done, will provide a chance for ripostes (see Chapter Eleven) angulated to the back or sides. Avoid monotonous or continual use of the same parries, unless you wish intentionally to condition your opponent and lure him into making an attack which underestimates your repertoire of parries.

Against compound attacks, you must make successive parries. These are some of the possibilities. Against a disengage-disengage (one-two) from sixte, you *could* parry quarte and sixte—two lateral parries. A better choice, however, would be the lateral to quarte and a counterquarte. You could also parry quarte and septime. And it is in this situation that a half-supination of the hand is preferred to a pronated hand. Against a disengage-disengage in quarte, you could parry sixte and countersixte. The chances and choices are equal as they are with sixte and octave.

When the feint is to the low line, your first parry could be octave or septime, but it should be accompanied by a fairly deep retreat. Try this out with a partner in very slow tempo. You will discover that your first response by a low parry will be easily deceived, especially if it is executed without a retreat.

The parries, in themselves, constitute the most single important element in the whole defensive system. When the sword evolved to the point that the blade itself was used for defense—rather than a shield, a dagger or cloak, sand thrown into the eyes, or armor—modern fencing was born.

DISTANCE

Keeping distance plays an important role in fencing—in defense and also in attack. In judging the distance, you must consider your opponent's speed, his height, his looseness in covering ground by the length of his steps forward or backward. The complete fencer must control the distance. Its manipulation is of great tactical importance. Distance is not measured from target to target, but is the distance between the point and the target.

A defending fencer is "out of distance" when a hit cannot be made by an attacker without his first executing a compound movement of the feet. If out of distance, an attacker cannot acquire the right of way until his point threatens a valid target. This situation presents tempo opportunities to the defender—until right of way is acquired. A step forward by the attacker may present the vigilant defender, sensitive to tempo, a moment in which to make a surprise attack. This kind of watchfulness pays off, but it is based on an understanding of, and a feel for, timing.

DISPLACEMENTS

The two body displacements described below have been borrowed from the Italian school of fencing. Hits scored by the use of body displacement moves are stop hits, because they are executed during the opponent's attack and are executed as defensive-offensive actions.

In Quartata (Side-step)

The in quartata is a defensive move that can be used when the attacking blade is directed to the inside line. Body and blade moves are executed simultaneously. Take a side-step diagonally to the outside by withdrawing the left leg to the right and rear. Your arm extension may direct your point to your opponent's low inside

In quartata

target area or follow a helical path to a high line and (purportedly) score a touch. Or you might move your opponent's blade in a croisé, *holding* it down in a horizontal position until your point arrives on target.

The in quartata is seldom used and its value is probably as a surprise move. It can be deceived, and this is probably why some fencing texts omit it. However, again, to be a complete fencer is to know the changes and innovations as they have evolved.

Passata Sotto (Ducking)

This body displacement should be employed *only* to defend against attacks made to a high line. The left foot is brought back and the unarmed hand placed on floor to form a tripod. The point stops the attacker in his tracks and his thrust passes overhead. If your opponent is much taller, you will probably be able to bend your knees and lower the trunk, rather than forming a tripod. In this

Passata sotto

case, you can gain some time in execution. Bear in mind that if the thrust lands on your mask, then you have substituted this invalid surface for a valid surface and the hit will be scored. Reread the material on the target in Chapter Three.

COUNTERATTACKS

The AFLA rule book defines counterattacks as "defensive-offensive actions." However, because they are executed during the attack, I group them under "defense."

Types of Counterattacks (Stop Hits)

There are two situations in which a counterattack might be used. We will consider counterattacks made in tempo situations and counterattacks made in opposition—the stop in time, the stop with opposition.

In certain instances, an opponent's attack may be executed in such a way that the defending fencer is given an opportunity to

A counter attack (stop hit), made by the vigilant defender (right) while opponent's point was off-target. Had the attack arrived it would have been scored, because the defender did not have right of way. The defender may be said to have "taken over" the attack, although this term does not appear in classical fencing literature.

make an offensive move within the tempo of the attack. It is essential that a counterattack of this sort be "in time." In these tempo actions, it is the point that is involved. In a nontempo situation, a counterattack may be made by "opposition," although it is still necessary that the time element be favorable. In opposing the oncoming blade, the point, blade, and guard are involved. Here there must be perfect execution in "closing" the line of attack. This counterattack was formerly called a "time thrust" or "time hit."

The Stop in Time

The AFLA rules state that "the stop in time is made with a period of fencing time." Keep in mind that a period of fencing time is not a fixed period of time which can be measured, but is rather the time necessary to execute a simple fencing action, and will vary from fencer to fencer. It follows therefore, and is the rule, that a

85

stop in time cannot be made against a simple attack executed in one period of fencing time. (This presupposes that the simple attack is fully developed with the threat continuous.) However, the stop will be valid when it arrives while the attacking point is off target, or is withdrawn during the attack. A perfect example is the stop hit made against a cut-over while the point is directed to the ceiling; or, while the attacking point is otherwise off target. See the illustration and reread the discussion of the cut-over and period of fencing time in Chapter Seven.

The stop would also be valid if it arrives ahead of the second blade movement in either a disengage-disengage, a straight thrust-disengage, a disengage-cut-over, or when it arrives ahead of the final movement of any multiple feint attack. Here, the requirement of the rule is complied with.

Another circumstance in which the stop would be valid is if it is made against an advance on a bent-arm attack. However, while it is true that an attack is characterized by an extended arm because it threatens the target, a director may determine that the bent arm did in fact constitute a threat and disallow the stop. It is also possible that the director may deem the bent arm to be an invitation and the opponent's stop as the initial attack.

Stop with Opposition

The AFLA rules state that the stop with opposition "is a counterattack executed while closing the line in which the opponent's attack will be terminated." This counterattack anticipates and intercepts the final movement of an attack. It does not require the precedence of a period of fencing time. It arrives in the same period of fencing time as the attack would have, had it not been intercepted.

For example, consider an attack by one-two (disengage-disengage) from either sixte or quarte. The defender, rather than using successive parries, could execute a stop by opposition. Here he would parry the first disengage (or make a false parry if he did in fact actually anticipate a one-two). However, instead of the second parry to deflect the second disengage, he would thrust his fist and whole blade diagonally across to the other line. By so doing, the open line would be closed and the deceiving blade intercepted, and the stop made. The diagonal move is continuous and forceful. The opposition stop thrust may also be made directly against a straight thrust.

Use of Counterattacks

Avoid getting into the habit of substituting counterattacks for parries, however. There are perils inherent in using them. First, as to the stop in time, some directors rarely or never permit such stop hits. The peril in a stop with opposition lies in the fact that there must be perfect execution of the opposition movement in closing the line. The opposition may also be too slow or may be precipitate. The choice in either stop is determined by the distance separating the fencers, the strength of the opponent's arm extension, and whether or not the movement is tentative or determined.

ATTACKS ON THE PREPARATION

An action founded on surprise and performed at the very moment your opponent is concentrating on his attack and before the attack has been fully developed is termed an attack on the preparation.

To seize the proper moment, you must maintain a state of constant vigilance and have the ability to manipulate distance against your opponent. You might (1) deceive by a disengage any attempted attack (beat or change-beat) on your blade; or (2) deceive on a first "taking" of your blade; or (3) take a step back to lure your distance-wise opponent to step *forward*, then launch your own attack *before* he has acquired the right of way; or (4) step forward unexpectedly against your opponent's advance, again before he has fully developed his attack and gained the right of way.

These terms are applicable to the above and you should know and use them: *Dérobement*, the *evasion* of an attack on your blade, is always performed by the defender. Examples (1) and (2) above are of dérobement. *Trompement*, a deceive performed by the attacker, deceives the opponent's parry.

87

Beat up — and hit to low line. A tactical action used against a fencer carrying hand too high in his thrust.

Occasionally, a fencer will notice that his opponent retreats but takes no action thereafter, doing so apparently just to survey the situation. As a tactic then, a fencer may remain on the lunge rather than return to guard immediately hoping to lure the opponent into a taking of his blade from which he will escape and can impale his opponent.

How would you classify this tactic? Is it a trompement or dérobement, or is the escape and impalement a counterattack , or is it a movement of second intention?

An attack on the preparation should not be confused with an attack made against or into an attack which already has the right of way.

chapter ten

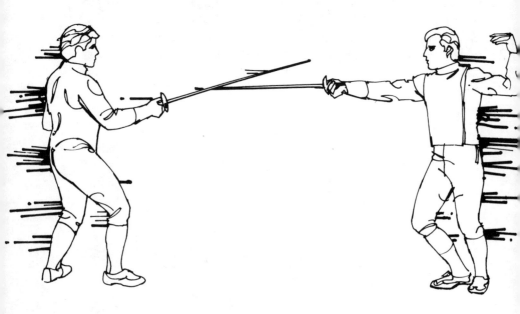

A compound, or composite attack, is made up of a combination of two or more simple attacks, one or more of which is a feint. The feint or feints are designed to draw a parry that is deceived by another blade movement. The feint therefore must always move just ahead of the parry or parries.

The beginning fencer need not learn any new strokes to execute a compound attack. He must learn, however, to coordinate his blade movements with his foot movements and to make his attacks progressive. In his progress, he will discover for himself, or should, that multiple feint attacks are extremely difficult to bring about successfully, that the risk of a counterattack increases with their use, and that multiple feints should be a subject of discussion or classification, rather than execution. Most good fencers limit their compound attacks to single feints.

compound attacks

The beginner should not use compound attacks until he or she has reached a reasonably good level of competency in the execution of simple attacks. It will then be much easier to coordinate and combine the various foot and blade movements for a successful compound attack. There is infinite satisfaction for both beginner and advanced fencer in scoring on a compound attack —in knowing that he has concealed his intention and misled the opponent to his disadvantage.

USE OF COMPOUND ATTACKS

Compound attacks are used when simple attacks don't succeed. You should understand why your simple attacks fail. Your defender may be naturally faster in his blade movements when parrying.

Figure 19. Attack by disengage-disengage (one-two). From an engagement in sixte (top) the fencer on right makes a feint disengage into quarte to draw opponent's lateral parry of quarte and deceives his opponent's parry by rounding his guard into the now open sixte line, where the hit is delivered (bottom).

And even if he does not have that advantage, defensive moves generally have a shorter travel distance than the point from which the attack is launched. It is this disadvantage that the compound attack erases, provided that the feint is executed with a lunge and the final thrust is also executed while on the lunge, the point always closing distance to the target uninterrupted and gaining time and distance. It is these factors that constitute a progressive attack.

Bear in mind that dexterity of point and point control (finger play) are essential to any success as a competitive fencer. They are especially necessary in executing a compound attack and are the reason why I have included exercises to develop this. (See Chapter Six.) You *must* have dexterity of point and point control in order to deceive or be ahead of the parries your feint has forced from your opponent. Should your opponent "find" (make contact with) your attacking blade during your feint, or feints, it will probably be deemed a parry by the director, and the right to riposte will be conferred.

Examples of compound attacks include a straight thrust as the feint, followed by a disengage; a disengage feint, followed by a disengage (one-two); a cut-over, followed by a disengage; and a disengage, followed by a cut-over.

Another possible compound attack is a double cut-over. This is difficult to execute, however, and places almost all fencers in considerable peril from the opponent's counterattack or counteraction into your tempo.

It is also possible to execute an attack by a double. In this case, the feint is usually made by a straight thrust or disengage and provokes a counter (circular) parry. The deceive is made by following the counter all the way around and ending in the same line as your disengage or straight thrust. The counter is made clockwise in sixte, your deceive is made counterclockwise (vice versa against the counter which is made from quarte). The feint here can be made by cut-over also but should you direct it to the inside (quarte) line, it is doubtful that your opponent will make a counterparry. You may deceive a change of engagement by double. Again, timing is all-important.

Figure 20. Attack by doublé. From an engagement in sixte (top) or from absence of blade, the fencer on right makes a feint disengage into quarte and deceives the defender's circle parry by following the circle around, counterclockwise. Lifting the blade point, the attacker delivers the hit into the now open quarte line (bottom).

CHECK LIST ON FEINTS

(1) Discover, as soon as possible, the cadence or speed of your opponent. This varies from fencer to fencer. Knowing the cadence, or changing your own, may enable you to deliberately break your compound attack. This change of rhythm, an exception to the rule of a progressive attack, could surprise your opponent.

(2) There is no absolute free will in attack. Its form will depend on your opponent's defense. His use of simple parries, lateral or half-circle, will limit your attack to disengagements or disengages and cut-overs. His use of successive parries, each in a different category, will dictate the form of your attack. Discover your opponent's parries, or patterns of parries, through the use of fast, simple attacks. Then move to the use of feint attacks.

Sometimes, however, you may have a hand in determining your opponent's moves. You may be able to induce your opponent to make a lateral or circle parry, or, at the very least, a lateral parry. Success here lies in the deliberate execution of a very wide but on-target straight thrust or disengage as a feint. The parry *must* be lateral—a circle parry will not work, because it will most likely oppose the foible to the forte and cannot properly deflect it. In fact, a circle parry in this case may very well deflect the blade more to the center of the target, helping it along. The lateral parry can then be more easily deceived by this feint because it has been anticipated. However, a narrow close to the guard straight thrust or disengage as a feint will more likely produce a circle parry, which can be deceived by a double. Here again you can more or less anticipate this parry, because you have first brainwashed your opponent with the wide, almost off-target feint. In competition, it is the winner who knows not only the rules but the exceptions.

(3) Most beginners, and some advanced fencers, are precipitate with the leading foot (out of "sync") in making their feints. Constant practice of multiple feints and great care in extending the arm before the foot movement or lunge will help in acquiring judgment and control and a better sense of tempo.

(4) A defender need not parry an off-target feint. Be careful that your attacks are properly executed in this regard. Be on target; threaten the target.

(5) Many beginners will withdraw the arm after a feint and before the final movement of the compound attack. This is because they are uncertain of being able to clear or "round" the opposing guard by a good disengage, to make the deceive effectively. This is destructive and the attacker is then subject to a stop in time. The remedy is simple: Keep the arm extended on the feint and then deceive; practice the finger-play exercises so that you *can* make the disengage while the arm is extended and you are on the lunge.

(6) It is entirely possible in a compound attack to make combinations of blade and foot movements in one period of fencing time *if they are performed simultaneously with the lunge.* Examples are beat and advance; beat, disengage, and so forth. These combinations of blade and foot movements are ways of introducing the compound attack.

(7) A feint may be made into any line. It may be made outside or inside, low or high, with the final of the attack into either outside or inside, high or low. Practice makes perfect but it is fun, too.

ON DECEIVES

You should practice deceives at each practice session. Take turns with a partner, practicing disengages from lateral and half-circle parries. On your partner's move across from sixte to quarte and back to sixte, your disengages should be small with the point making a small "U." Your partner should alternate from lateral to circle parries. Of course, your disengages or deceives are accomplished by finger play, as are your doubles against his counterparries. These exercises will aid in the ability to deceive the parry while you are on the lunge. You may take the on-guard stance (but standing erect) for these exercises, if you wish.

chapter eleven

A riposte is the offensive action made by a fencer who has parried an attack. A counterriposte is the offensive action made by the fencer who has parried a riposte (or counterriposte). The right to execute these offensive movements is conferred by the execution of a parry, under the right-of-way rule.

This right to riposte may not be accepted by the defender; therefore, ripostes are characterized as being immediate or delayed (temps perdu). When a riposte has been delayed, the right of way is lost and the original attacker may initiate a renewal of his attack. Beginning fencers, as a general rule, often fail to riposte. More often than not, they will retreat out of distance or hold the parry. They are advised to consider the parry and the following riposte as a single unit of fencing action—and to practice parry-riposte exercises as single actions. Their retreats should be deliberate—either to

the riposte
and counterriposte

survey the bout situation (a regrouping of forces) or to run out the remaining time when ahead on touches. For the advanced fencer, the choice to retreat may be dependent upon the fencing actions of his opponent.

RIPOSTES

The Simple Riposte

In addition to being characterized as immediate or delayed, a riposte may be simple or compound in nature. As with the simple attack, the *simple riposte* consists of a single blade movement and may be either direct or indirect. The direct riposte is made in the same line as the parry by straight thrust or a graze along the blade. The indirect riposte is made by either a disengage or cut-over.

Figure 21. In the direct riposte, the attack is parried by lateral parry of quarte (top), and the riposte begun with defender on left dipping his point directly toward target (center); he then delivers the riposte by a mere arm extension — a straight thrust riposte (bottom).

Figure 22. In the indirect riposte, the attack is parried by lateral parry of quarte (top). Riposte begins with defender passing his blade *under* attacker's blade, covering the quarte line (center). The defender then deceives rounding attacker's guard and delivers the riposte in sixte line (bottom).

The Compound Riposte

As with the compound attack, the compound riposte consists of two or more blade movements, one or more of which is a feint. The feint or combination of feints may be either a straight thrust, a disengage, or a cut-over. The compound riposte should usually not comprise more than a single feint. When multiple feints are used, whether by the attacker or by the defender, they have a limiting effect on both fencers. The blade could be found by the opponent; instinctive, undisciplined actions are more likely to be performed; positions of the hand and blade could be seriously altered; the distance itself might not be properly utilized. The implications are many.

The Delayed Riposte

There is some tactical justification for the advanced fencer to delay his or her riposte. It does allow a moment to observe the blade movements of the opponent returning to guard after his unsuccessful attack, or in which to observe his general characteristics, such as arm or body movement or positions—and, to act accordingly thereafter.

RENEWAL OF ATTACKS

There are three *traditional* methods by which a fencer may renew his or her attack. They are secondary offensive moves and subject to performance by either an attacker or a riposter.

The Remise

To execute a remise, the point is replaced on target while on the lunge in the line in which the parry is made and executed without an additional blade movement. The remise is used against an opponent who (1) makes a bad parry and fails to riposte; (2) parries and holds the parry, delaying his riposte; (3) parries and executes a compound riposte. In the last case, the remise must be ahead of the final movement to obtain right of way.

The Redoublement

The redoublement, also executed while on the lunge, differs from the remise in that the replacement is preceded by a second movement of the blade or arm. It is used against a failure to riposte.

The Reprise of Attack

A renewal of attack made immediately after a return to guard, forward or to the rear, is a reprise of attack.

In today's fencing, renewed attacks are often made in combination with whatever foot movements are necessary to achieve the touch. The renewed actions are made with extended but not locked-in arm. The thrust is usually angular. If the distance permits, many fencers will renew their attacks by cut-over.

COUNTERRIPOSTES

When the fencing phrase includes a series of movements, from the initial attack through to counterripostes, the beginning fencer is very likely to indulge in what may prove to be uncontrolled, slashing blade movements, subjecting himself to counterattacks at several points along the way. A mere withdrawal of his arm, with the point off-target is in itself evidence that the fencer has lost control of the bout situation. Swift, simple or single feint offensive actions are the most effective, whether attacker or riposter.

An advanced fencer may consider a counterriposte as a second intention. He will stay on the lunge, usually parry the riposte, and score on his counterriposte. This premeditated offensive action is used against an opponent who parries well, and the expectation is to draw the return parry and then counterriposte, catching the opponent unprepared. Against the riposte of an opponent who has speed and is precise with his point, the counterriposter will either parry the return during a recovery to guard with appel (a quick stamp of the foot), or shift his body weight to the rear, and then make his counterriposte.

For classification and reference, the attacker's counterriposte is known as the first counterriposte, and the parry and return thrust is known as the second counterriposte (by the original defender). The attacker's counterripostes are odd-numbered, the defender's are even-numbered. A phrase could conceivably go to eight or nine or more counterripostes.

Basically, in executing a riposte or counterriposte, the defender may perform whatever actions that would have been open if he had been the original attacker. The limitations imposed, however, are identical to the limitations imposed on the attacker. So also are the requirements.

These limitations and requirements arise out of, and stem from, the rules and practices governing the performance of all fencing actions. They have been developed (and revised) for centuries. The beginner should study the following paragraph point-by-point, and keep the information in his mind's eye, so to speak, as a brief, integrated presentation of the sport. This will counteract the fragmentation that occurs in most fencing literature. I believe the beginner will then acquire a quicker and more complete understanding of the sport. Understanding leads to progress.

First and foremost, it is essential to remember that fencing is a game of alternating action between attacker and defender. The fencers must observe the phrase d'armes (the fencing phrase) and it is the duty of the director to see that the phrase "be followed through." This means that the attack must be correctly executed, that the defender must parry (or completely avoid the attack), that the return thrust (riposte) must also be correctly executed. The phrase is *not* followed through when the attacker withdraws his arm during the attack, or attacks into a point-in-line without first deflecting it, or when he attacks into an attack. The phrase is *not* followed through on the part of the defender if he chooses to counterattack without the benefit of a cadence (or tempo) or period of fencing time. The phrase is observed if he "finds" the attacker's blade on a feint. This would be deemed a parry.

Keep in mind that an action or actions deemed valid by the director—those which result in a touch—terminate the phrase. Also, remember that under the concept of alternating action, there is an orderly system of play, the foundation for which is the right of way. This right is maintained or lost by correctly or incorrectly ex-

A riposte from prime parry. Attacker (right) either failed or was slow to return to guard; the riposter stepped in, displacing his body, and made the hit.

ecuting the various actions we choose to perform *under all the rules.*

Secondly, under the right-of-way rule, if a counterattack, correctly made in time or by opposition, results in a touch, the touch will be scored. Here also the phrase terminates.

When we integrate in our minds all these fragments as they are presented in fencing literature, then we will truly understand the meaning of phrase d'armes and be able to see that the phrase must be followed through.

chapter twelve

W hether you fence to improve personal discipline, for pleasure, or with total dedication, you should be aware of some of the problems, conventions, and advances in competitive fencing.

For the novice fencer, the first competitive bout will probably be in an AFLA-sponsored meet or in an interclub affair. He or she will first be plagued by the question of choices—whether to take the attack or to defend (take the attack!). What should one do if the opponent also decides to attack or if the opponent is faster; or if the jury is deaf, dumb, and blind. These same dilemmas have been presented since the beginning of time. It seems that the first thing beginners do is forget everything they have learned. Facing up to an unknown, completely uncooperative fencer, with no team members to cover for you, can be traumatic. But it need not be, if you use your head. Some practical tips on tactics may help.

competition

TACTICS

Observe Your Opponent

First of all, you must know the basics. Before you are called to fence, observe other fencers in their bouts. Take note of the favorite patterns of each fencer, his or her failure or observance of good fundamentals, especially these!

Does he really lunge in delivering his attacks or does he merely reach out in his effort to hit? The reacher usually does not make a hit. In this case, watch your distance. Keep it! You can win with a sense of distance. Also, you should lunge yourself, and don't forget to get your arm out there.

Does your opponent parry and fail to reposte? One answer is to remise or redouble. Another is to consciously follow each of your own parries with a riposte. Don't retreat out of distance making the riposte impossible without some fancy footwork, which you may or may not perform. Why waste effort?

Does the opponent attack into other attacks? This action may be prompted by your opponent's attack and therefore would be behind your action. In this case, he does not have the right of way. The director may not see it that way and call it "simultaneous" rather than giving the attacker the hit. Against this kind of fencer, you should win if you use your head. Provoke these moves by making a very sincere but actually *false* attack, with a short step or half-lunge; you are then prepared to parry the attack and follow with a successful scoring move. Here, your first intention was to provoke the second intention to score on the parry and riposte.

Relax

Consciously try to contain your excitement. Restrain yourself from making instinctive and impulsive moves. There is no need to respond to every move of your opponent, although it is important to be constantly alert. The only secret I know of in fencing is the secret of controlling the excitement. You can acquire this secret—but you must work at it.

Specific Tactics

Opponent has high guard:
    a.   Attack into low line
    b.   Beat up and attack low
    c.   Feint low—deceive parry and hit high
Opponent has low guard:
    a.   Attack high line
    b.   Cut-over to high line
Opponent continually stop-hits:
    a.   Make simple attacks
    b.   Make false attacks and
    c.   Bind (provoke the stop)

Opponent is (much) shorter:
    a. Keep the measure
    b. Stop hit
Opponent is (much) taller:
    a. Use the "gain"
    b. Be cautious in advancing
    c. Use the second intention
Opponent is left-handed:
    a. The usual advice is to fence against a lot of left-handers, but you may never get the chance. If *you* are left-handed, then your opponent has the same problem.
    b. Attack to his outside low line (his octave). Usually, he will be weak in parrying shots to the outside lines. Feint to what are usually his strong parries (inside lines) and end your offense to his octave.
    c. Keep in a good sixte and execute countersixte parries.
    d. Observe as many left-handed fencers as you can.

A Final Word on Tactics

Tactics and techniques should be considered by all fencers as the song about love and marriage did—"You can't have one without the other." The first axiom in fencing is to hit and not be hit. Knowing and understanding the multiplicity and diversity of fencing actions, the methods of execution available and their application in competition constitute the necessary ingredients for the successful fencer. However, perfect execution of these actions is equally important. The correct tactical move or the correct technical action could fail through poor execution.

ELECTRIC FOIL

A relatively recent advance in terms of fencing competition is the electric foil—a system whereby touches can be electronically scored, releasing the fencer from the tyranny of a judge. This system is not without its disadvantages, however, and during the early years of use; it led to sloppy fencing.

Fencer wears a metallic vest used in electric foil fencing.

Early Use

During what I call the first period of electric foil, directors did not understand the system and relied on it exclusively rather than combining it with their own good judgment. This confusion led to a sloppy, pig-sticking style of fencing. In their ignorance (not shared by their Eastern European counterparts), many directors would not give right of way to the immediate riposte; instead they gave it to the attacker who continued his attack after the parry and, touching a target, set off a colored light. As is obvious now, the touch should have been given to the riposter.

We are now in the second period of electric fencing, a return to a more classical form and technique and a better understanding of the machine's function. Precedence and right of way are now given to the immediate riposte, all else being equal. Also present in this second period of electric fencing are fencing actions that are much more complex and diverse than in the first period. Improvement in equipment and a growing understanding have made this possible.

In the first period, electric foils were much too flexible and whippy; the retractable point put too much weight at the tip. When I first used the electric foil and made a disengage from an engagement in sixte, for example, the point whipped out far from the target and had to be replaced in line in order for the thrust to score. I was forced to fence with absence of blade and reduce my game to much more simple actions, as was everyone else.

Electric Foil Fencing Today

The second period began with the introduction of an improved point and a less whippy blade. Classical form and more complex actions became possible. As a matter of fact, in some ways we have gone back even farther to some actions which had become obsolete in standard foil. This is evidenced in part by an increasing use of the obsolete parries of prime and quinte. See illustrations.

Still, many differences remain between electric foil and nonelectric fencing. They arise for the most part from the fact that the machine "sees" hits formerly unseen by human, and sometimes biased, jurors.

There is, therefore, no doubt in my mind that we are approaching a third period of electric-foil fencing. The following are some specifics which characterize today's electric-foil fencing.

Advanced fencers are now inclined to use a revolver grip. (It is a mistake for beginners.) There is frequent use of "second intention."

There is special emphasis on attack and the continuations of the attack. These continuations (or renewals) are characterized by frequent use of cut-overs and angular replacements to carry out the renewal. The angular replacement is used against the defender whose retreat is insufficient or whose parry does not close the line adequately, or who does not follow his inadequate parry with a second parry. The cut-over may be parried with the foil quinte parry shown in the illustration. The speed of execution of the cut-over prompts its use where the defender has combined retreat with a parry. There are also longer phrases, a phrase continuing as far as a counterparry riposte. Fencers are "carrying" the weapon more effectively—showing an improvement in awareness of the different parts of the blade. Thrusts or actions are being made from positions not usual in standard foil or in the first period of electric foil.

There is almost equal use of counterattacks and parries. Foot movements are increasingly efficient—in preparation for manipulation of distance or in combination with hand movements for improved coordination. A large variety of combinations are also being used.

The International Scene

During the first period of the electric foil, many United States coaches and fencing masters described the changes as being "revolutionary." They were wrong. Their conclusions were made because, at that time, Americans were suffering from almost total defeat at the hands of Eastern European nations. Their simple and more athletic game and the extensive use of renewed attacks, among other so-called innovations, opposed to our attempt to mix standard and electric-foil techniques, led us down a primrose path.

We are doing much better now. Many of our international fencers acquit themselves better than ever before, and have drawn high praise from foreign masters and fencers. The efforts of the AFLA have been gargantuan, especially from the mid-1950s to the present, and they are continuing. Headed by elected officers without pay, the sincerity and dedication of these individuals have been something special. Our progress has not been without considerable travail and personal agony on the part of these men. The cooperation between the AFLA and the National Fencing Coaches Association of America, also augurs well for the future.

We should all know and realize the problems—those of the recent past and those which still exist—of competing on the international level.

Fencers from Eastern Europe start as young children, at eight to ten years, and many are completely subsidized from that time to the end of their competitive careers. They have unlimited time for training and competition. Salaries are given and all expenses paid. These fencers travel and compete frequently with top athletes from other countries, a decided advantage. Eastern Europeans have a large pool of professional coaches, facilities, equipment, trainers, and physicians from which to draw.

Those countries outside the Iron Curtain who also subsidize sports enjoy a greater share of victories. In some, within the capitalistic system, national coaches are appointed and government-paid. If nothing else is done, at least uniformity in methods of training, learning, and coaching are achieved.

However, the difficulties in the United States fencing arena are great. Our athletes start their careers at a more advanced age. Many encounter the sport for the first time in college. These fencers must develop at their own expense and on their own time. They pay for their own instruction, club fees, travel expenses to competitions, entry fees, equipment cost, and repair. Budding careers in business, the professions, or trades simply cannot be interrupted continually for training and conditioning. When in training, usually after working hours, our men establish and follow their own disciplines. It is by their own free will that they score their accomplishments.

AFLA's increasing efforts to broaden our fencing base appear to be meeting with some success. This is evidenced by the growing membership, especially in the younger age groups. This is also proven by our international successes in swimming, track and field, tennis and other sports, where instruction and training begin at six to ten years of age. The successes of other nations have also been achieved by this approach.

Many U.S. communities are now providing facilities in which to fence and give instruction for nominal fees. And, they are drawing the very young by appropriate promotion to parents in the local media. Within the last year, for instance, six Chicago suburbs added fencing to their sports and recreation programs. This did not just happen. The officials in these suburbs were approached by fencers, but their responses were immediate.

Many of our top fencers started at age fourteen in high school and reached top level at the time of graduation. Had they started at ten or eight, many of these could have reached international status.

We must discontinue the pointing of fingers at a lack of coaching, poor physical conditioning, a small fencing base, poor attitudes, lack of practice, lack of money, improper selection of Olympic representatives, and so on. Continued cooperation between AFLA activities and the activities of the National Fencing Coaches Association of America augur well for the future.

chapter thirteen

Although the foil is the most popular fencing weapon today, competition and training are available in two other weapons, the épée and sabre. We have included a minimal treatment of these weapons to give the potential student an idea of what is involved. However, this section is not intended for advanced competitors.

INTRODUCTION

Épée

The épée is a descendant of the short sword. It was developed for use in schools for duelists when it became apparent that the foil, with its mask and rules, made it unsuitable for a duel, as the wounding of an adversary was the sole consideration. Full development of the épée came after the middle of the last century.

épée

Sabre

The sabre differs from the foil and épée in that it is also a cutting weapon and touches are made by cutting, and by thrusting with the point. It descended from the curved cavalry sabre derived from the scimitar and introduced by the Hungarians late in the eighteenth century. The fencing sabre (it can also be a dueling weapon) was introduced by the Italians late in the nineteenth century. Its light weight enabled the sabreur to control it, and to build up swift and complex movements into phrases that made bouts a delight for the spectator.

In the early 1930s, the Hungarians introduced a new school or method of sabre fencing. This was largely the result of efforts by Italian fencing masters led by the famous Italo Santelli, who moved

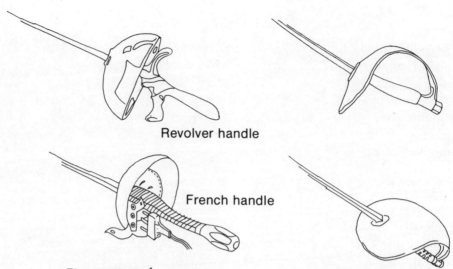

Revolver handle

French handle

Figure 23. Epée handles   Figure 24. Sabres

to Hungary in the late 1890s. These efforts systematized the Hungarian style of sabre fencing. Hungarian sabre fencers displaced the Italian school almost completely and they have dominated world sabre competitions ever since. A fencer could walk into the middle of a top level sabre competition and recognize the Hungarians by their fencing style.

Today, the Hungarian school of sabre fencing is bumping into the Soviet system. Soviet sabre-fencing fundamentals have been, in almost all areas, borrowed or taken from the Hungarian and do not differ much from them. The two schools, however, are in some ways different and seem to be vying for supremacy with victory going sometimes to one and sometimes to the other. In my opinion, the scores have not yet been fully tallied; they may well seesaw back and forth for some time.

HINTS AND CAUTIONS

Fencers are, for the most part, an inquisitive lot. Some, in clubs or groups, will purchase sabre and épée weapons and play around with them with no idea of their proper use. While foilists will do much better in épée with no instruction (and some do very well), they will usually fare poorly with the sabre. And many, with no idea of competing or developing themselves in the weapon, slash away at each other. Not only do they inflict body welts but they also can dangerously damage a foil mask leaving deep impressions and breaking or nearly breaking the wire. Upon resuming foil practice, perhaps that very same day or evening, these individuals may be fencing with a defective and dangerous mask.

FENCING WITH THE ÉPÉE

The épée is often referred to as a realistic weapon, because of the similarity of épée fencing to dueling. The attempt to closely emulate the duel years ago by fencing for one touch, and then several, failed, because the bouts were extremely dull. Much caution—but not much fencing—resulted. Today, épée competitions are fenced for five or sometimes ten touches, and electric scoring apparatus is nearly always used. Épée competitions without electric scoring are still dull and uninteresting to my mind.

Comparisons of Épée and Foil

In a very basic way, certain techniques of fencing are said to be common to all three weapons. With some modifications, similarities between épée and foil include the stance, foot and leg movements, manipulation of the point, ability to carry the weapon, the sense of distance, tempo and feel for the bout situations. Both épée and foil are thrusting weapons and touches are scored only by the point.

There are two main differences between épée and foil. Épée has no right-of-way rule (foil and sabre do); and the épée's target is the fencer's entire body and his clothing and equipment. In both these respects, the similarity between épée and duel is seen. Without the right-of-way convention, it is a question of who hits first and the maxim "hit and don't be hit" becomes very important. The hand and arm now become vulnerable to hits.

Without Right of Way

With no priority for the attack (no right-of-way rule or

117

Figure 25. Epée target

convention) it is, of course, possible for those using épées to score touches on each other at about the same time. The scoring machine signals a double touch if the time between the two touches is between 1/20th and 1/25th of a second. If there is a double touch and both touches are valid, the two fencers are counted as touched. Without a scoring machine, the director decides if there was a difference in time sufficient to confer priority, or if there was a double touch. If he has no opinion, he must declare a double touch. This also supports the contention that épée fencing does in effect emulate the duel.

Other differences between épée and foil concern corps-à-corps (bodily contact) and the weapon itself. In an épée bout, a competitor may, by flèche or determined advances, cause a corps-à-corps several times in succession.If done without either brutality or violence, the fencer has not violated the fundamental conventions and is not guilty of any irregularity. In a foil bout, corps à corps may draw warnings and penalties. As for the weapons, the weight and flexibility of the blades are different and the épée has an enlarged guard. You should keep this in mind whenever fencing

118

A toe attack. This hit is possible only in épée, because the target is the fencer's entire body. However, a toe attack can be mounted only against an inattentive fencer; the fencer on left should have made a stop hit to the attacker's hand or wrist.

épée, even in practice. The French handle for épée corresponds to the foil handle but is slightly larger in the grip. It is held in a more supinated position.

THE ON-GUARD AND STANCE

Modifications in the épée on-guard position lead to better protection of the entire body. The feet are at right angles but closer together than in foil, because too wide a stance leaves the fencer open to a hit in the foot or knee. The fencer holds the weapon in sixte, as in foil, but lowers the point to just below the hand and extends his arm slightly.

It is more important to close the outside lines (sixte and octave), to prevent exposure of the shoulder, elbow, or inside of the arm. Cover (as shown in the sketch) your hand and lower arm in back of the guard; keep them pointed in the same direction.

The trunk is more erect in the épée lunge, but presents the same profile as in foil. This is an attempt to avoid hits on the mask; but is probably observed more in the breach than in the practice. In your lunge, keep the hand at shoulder height. Imagine that a magnet on the target is drawing your point—your hand and forearm in line.

The Measure and Distance

The fencing measure in épée traditionally is such that with a full lunge, you can hit your adversary in the middle of his forearm, and with a half-lunge, hit on his wrist. In modern épée, however, many more attacks are scored on the chest. This seems to be the result of a fencing system developed by the Hungarians. But, at this writing, it is almost impossible to be exact.

In considering distance, quarter your opponent's guard and keep in mind that his hand is behind the lower outside quadrant. It is not necessary to see this "advanced target" to score a hit there; angulate and aim to just miss the guard. This could give bonus touches if kept in mind. Also, his hand may drift, presenting another opportunity.

Footwork

Mobility, with shorter, rapid steps are key words for the épéeist. Also, the effectiveness of the flèche is greater in épée than in foil. Each of these, the lunge and the flèche, are performed dynamically but with control, and in taking the blade, as in a press or pressure, with opposition.

Defense and Attack

Defense is tied rather closely to attack in épée, because the épéeist does not parry if his opponent's target is exposed in reach. This may not be too bad a gamble considering the time interval is favorable.

Parries

Defense is relatively simple, with the object to deflect offensive actions to the outside of the sword arm. Lateral parries have an in-

The épéeist does not parry if his opponent's target is in reach. In the situation above, the fencer on the right, when attacked, made a stop hit to the top of his opponent's arm.

herent risk in that they expose a target. Counter and half-circle parries are much safer, if technically well done. Do not alternate parries; your opponent will soon catch on. Avoid all set sequences. Angular thrusts made to the hand or wrist are usually parried by opposing the guard to the attacking point.

Épée parries may be taken by opposition or by beat. On attacks to the inside high line, a final quarte parry performed as in foil will permit your opponent to redouble against your riposte, presenting a double touch situation. Where the score is four to three against you, the double touch will cost you the bout.

In college fencing, a coach may decide on the spot to have a foilist fence on the épée team hoping for better distribution of strength, even though the foilist has never fenced in that weapon. I have had to do this many times and sometimes I won and

Fencer on left makes an opposition thrust in sixte against an attack.

sometimes I lost. And this depended on general temperament of the fencer. It's rather easy to spot the situation of foilist versus épéeist. The foilist may get away with a quarte parry and riposte successfully, if he remembers to make it by opposition or does so by accident. Team members of the épéeist will spot this immediately (and the fencer himself perhaps while still engaged in the bout). And then, the experienced épéeist will make the very first action a feint to the high inside line, draw the big quarte parry, and hit the then exposed target—hand, wrist, or forearm. Watching this can be very funny.

Therefore, on attacks to this line, keep your hand in sixte, beat the opposing blade and riposte again with opposition. On attacks from close in, parry by opposition. Successive parries of quarte and counterquarte may be used occasionally. But don't make a habit of responding to feints in quarte. The idea is to vary your parries and to fence as simply as possible. Be orthodox; follow the

Against an attack in sixte (top), the fencer on left uses a beat parry and ripostes to the inside forearm (bottom).

An example (here and facing page) of a taking of the blade used successfully.

book and don't deviate until you understand the basics of épée technique. Unorthodox épéeists are constant losers.

Attacks against the knee or foot are met with a stop thrust to either the wrist or forearm or to the mask, whichever target is closest. The stop is executed by retracting the leading foot, heel to heel, straightening the legs (also known as reassembling), and

Against an extended arm, the fencer on right takes the opposing blade, lifts it, and steps in to score a hit in octave.

thrusting. The thrust is made immediately with the retraction and is usually accompanied by a slight inclination of the body.

Defenses Against Preparations for Attack

Usually defenses against preparations for attack occur within the

125

framework or structure discussed at length in the foil text. Beats, pressures, and takings of the blade (binds, prises-de-fer) are used frequently in épée fencing.

Keep in mind, as a defender, however, the following three considerations. First, a good épéeist uses beats and pressures primarily as a surprise or shock tactic and refrains from overuse. Second, the fencer takes the blade quite frequently so that after some experience, one should be able to measure to a good degree the frequency of these actions and govern oneself accordingly. Third, these attacking actions are performed against an extended arm (point in line). Knowing the form of these actions and the conditions of their use should enable you, as a defender, to cope with greater success.

Thinking defensively only and not tactically, the action to employ against attacks on the blade or taking of the blade is the dérobement. The dérobement is executed by completely evading the attacking blade (no contact), or by a yielding parry—exactly as described in Chapter Nine. Should you evade against a beat and lunge, or a beat and flèche, your opponent could very well impale himself on your still extended blade. Against a bind, or taking of your blade, you may yield and then disengage off the increasing pressure and stop hit with opposition; or you may yield to the appropriate guard position and riposte, again by opposition. Many épéeists have made respectable showings through repeated use of dérobements, often basing their whole game on this action. But that is a mistake. It is much better to have a complete game. Know the action and use it appropriately against constant attacks on your blade and against repetitive takings of your blade. On the other hand, when you take your opponent's blade and he avoids, mix the direction of your binds from clockwise to counterclockwise, until you can control his blade and properly deflect it. Further, combine your prise-de-fer with an advance. This will make an evasion more difficult.

Counter Time

"Counter time describes every action made by an attacker against his opponent's stop." This is an action of second intention, and the most efficient tactic against the stop hit. The stop hit is drawn or provoked by a feint, or false attack, or by a step forward or backward. The stop hit is then parried and the riposte follows. Or, with the stop hit, the attacker maintains his extended arm, angulates and thrusts with opposition. Many fencers and many coaches consider the proper application and use of counter time as effective as any action of offense or defense.

A BRIEF SUMMATION

1. Attack with the hand and arm behind the guard, the point threatening.
2. Remise or redouble immediately when you miss or if your opponent parries and does not immediately riposte. Redouble by disengage whenever you feel a contact or pressure against your blade.
3. Stop hit whenever your opponent does not cover behind the guard.
4. Fence with absence of blade.
5. Bear in mind *not* to parry your opponent's feints, that the épée-ist who parries every feint is usually the easiest to cope with— *unless you are able to discover* that his parries are premeditated to trick or deceive, and you are able to pick up his attack which follows.
6. Use a variety of cadences; do not withdraw the arm during your attack or in executing a renewal of attack.
7. Fence as *simply* as possible; avoid wide movements such as a cut-over. Pivot around your opponent's wrist or hand.

chapter fourteen

The proper grasp of the sabre is with the first joint of the thumb on the upper part of the hilt just below the metal hilt ring; and the first joint of the forefinger below or opposite. The middle fingers are bent over to help grasp the hilt. The palm is empty. In the initial or basic guard position, called tierce, the cutting edge of the blade is turned to the right with the wrist, and the hand is in pronation.

The sabre stance is almost identical with that of foil, although subject to some adjustment in respect to width of stance, body position, shifting of weight from one foot to another and so on. The left hand is placed on the left hip and remains there throughout, rather than being carried as it is in foil. Some beginners may honor this rule more in the breach than in strict observance.

sabre

FUNDAMENTAL POSITIONS

There are five sabre positions—numbered one to five. Two of them, the positions of prime and seconde are considered by some as secondary positions as are the parries taken in these positions. However, as a beginner, you should know them all and not be confronted with a surprise later on.

The first position is that of prime. In assuming the position, bend the arm at your elbow, lowering the point to knee height; turn the guard and move it to the left side so that it is in front of, and very slightly below, the level of the shoulder. The edge of the blade should be turned slightly to the left, with the point forward and bisecting a line between the feet as they are placed when on guard. The fist now before the shoulder, the forearm and upper

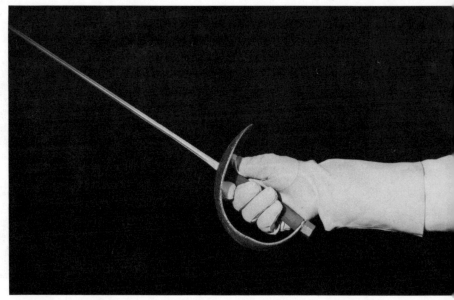

Proper sabre grip

arm form an obtuse (slight) angle in a horizontal plane. This position protects the left side of the body from shoulder to hip. The end position for a parry in prime is shown in an illustration.

The second position is that of seconde. To assume this position, lower the arm and point, move the fist to the right so that the top edge of the guard is slightly below shoulder level and to the right of the shoulder line. The arm and blade slant downward with the point aimed at the middle of your adversary's thigh. This position covers and protects the flank from hip to shoulder. The end position of a parry in seconde is shown in an illustration.

The third position is that of tierce. This position is the basic on-guard position and protects the flank, the arm, and the right cheek. The arm is bent at the elbow in front of the hip. The elbow should be about a hand span *away* from the hip. The blade points upward and forward diagonally at eye level and slightly to the right of the eye line. The blade should be in such a position so as to protect the arm and right cheek. The parry itself also protects the

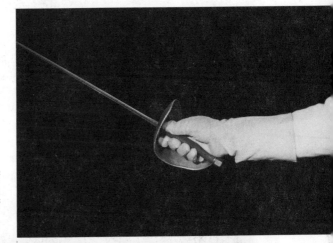

Side view (below) of tierce guard (Picture on right shows close-up of hand position).

flank. From this position, the fencer should be able to initiate his attack, a thrust or cut, from either a mobile or immobile situation as required. Fencers may assume a position with point in line or from seconde. This is dependent on the bout situation, the extent of and kind of preparation intended.

The fourth position is that of quarte. The elbow, again, is about a hand span out from the body, the guard in line with the left hip. The pommel is about the height of the hip line. The elbow itself is usually in front of the right thigh bone. This varies with physical conformation. The idea is to give as little exposure as possible to the right arm from an attack which might be made there. This position protects the left cheek, the chest, and abdomen. The cutting edge of the blade is turned to the left diagonally and forward with point up in relation to the body. The illustration shows the end position for a parry in quarte.

The fifth position is that of quinte (see illustration). The sabre is raised from tierce position to the height of the forehead so as to afford protection to cuts aimed at the head. The guard should be to the right of the right temple, a distance equal to the width of the palm. The forearm should lean forward slightly, on a small diagonal. The forte of the blade should be placed so as to form a right angle to any attacking blade, the point forward.

In forming this position and parry from tierce, the blade point should be dropped sufficiently so as to catch and gather the cut to the head from below. If the quinte parry is formed so that the point and blade are carried in a large arc, then the attacking blade will probably be below your attempted parry. It is your cutting edge, again, that is presented to the opposing blade.

Once you learn these positions and start to fence, you will find that the frequency of their use varies. However, do not be led astray and confine your practice to favored or frequently used positions. You should be proficient in them all. To do otherwise would be a mistake. If you are a complete novice, I suggest that it would be best for you to learn the positions in this order: tierce, quarte, quinte, seconde and then prime. The novice can get by with the first three, and many developing fencers do. As you progress, move on to seconde and prime.

Front view of position of tierce.

Figure 26. Sabre target

The blade movements going from one position to another or returning from one to another are referred to as transitions or passages. Some examples of transitions are from tierce to quarte, the guard moving horizontally to the left and right; from seconde to prime and back, the guard moving in a horizontal plane to left and right; and from seconde to quinte and back, the guard moving in a perpendicular plane. It is essential that the execution of these movements be initiated with the blade point and then continued immediately as a turn of the cutting edge with the fingers and from the wrist. Do not move the elbow more than necessary. Also, do not whip from the wrist; you must control the blade. These injunctions apply to the execution of all cuts and parries, as well as in the making of the transitions.

Thrusts and Cuts

The target for sabre is everything above the waist. The hits in sabre are made not only with the point—a straight thrust—but also with the front or back edge of the blade, called a cut. The cuts are made with a striking movement, with the last inch (or two) of the blade.

Front and side views of lunge with cut to head.

The straight thrust is usually made from tierce position. With the thumb and forefinger and a turning of the wrist, in pronation, the point is lowered in the direction of the thrust and the arm is then extended so as to form an obtuse angle.

Cuts are delivered to the flank, right cheek, the head, the left cheek, the chest, and to the lower and upper arm, either to the outside or inside of the arm. Point attacks may be delivered to the arm, body, and head. The point and cutting edge should make the hit before the heel of the lunging foot has touched the floor.

Distance

Three distances are used in sabre. A short distance is one from which you can reach your opponent's body with only one arm movement. The middle distance is one from which you can reach your opponent with either a step or lunge, and one arm movement. The long distance is a distance from which you can reach your opponent with a step, a lunge, and an arm movement. You should practice all the sabre actions from each distance.

Right of Way

Sabre fencing is governed by the same rules and conventions as govern foil. The target is larger, however, and because it is cut and thrust, sabre fencing has a special flavor all its own.

A new regulation governing simultaneous attacks in sabre may be put into effect in the near future. It is being considered because there are too many "simultaneous attacks," which lead to deadly dull sabre fencing. The new rule is designed to correct this situation.

THE ATTACKS

In general, attacks may be classified as either direct or compound (composite) and are made with either the point or the blade edge. Direct attacks do not involve any deception, i.e., they are not introduced by a feint, made to draw a parry which is deceived. They should be made with speed and in a straight line without hesitation. Direct attacks in sabre made by cut have a greater chance to

136

Point attack

succeed than the direct or simple attacks in foil, because in sabre, the target area is larger and the defender must make wider defensive moves.

Compound attacks involve the making of one or more feints. To be effective, a feint must contain the same sincerity as is shown in a simple, one-move attack; it must force the opponent to parry, which of course is deceived. The cut or thrust is then delivered to the target exposed in the parry. The beginner should limit the complexity of his attacking game to single feints or infrequent double feints—no more—except in practice, where multiple feints are used to acquire blade control and blade direction. Feints should be deep, bringing the blade as close as possible to the target.

Compound attacks should be made progressively, as explained in Chapter Ten. Foot movements should always be practiced in conjunction with the lunge in both simple and composite attacks. They should be short and rapid, with the body held erect. Attacks should be preceded by a preparation.

All sabre attacks and guard positions, such as tierce, quarte and seconde, should be executed or maintained so as to secure maximum protection from the guard. This can be achieved by practice—in lowering or raising the hand as required or by turning it to the right or left. Too much either way will expose the hand or cuff. Experiment with one of your fellows, taking turns from tierce and quarte at cutting with both fore edge and back edge at any exposure. You may find that the forearm is also exposed by only a slight variation in the position or location of the guard. When you find that too many hits are made at these limited but vulnerable targets, change the position of the guard. The application of simple logic should lead you to that position which affords maximum protection. Because of differing physical conformations, what is a good position for you may not be a good position for your partner. Bear in mind that parries are made with the cutting edge, and that presentation of the cutting edge is made by finger play and not by the heel of the sword hand.

Proper positioning of the guard and hand has a doubly significant relationship to cuts or point attacks made to the hand or arm. Not only should your hand be correctly positioned in all your attacking movements, but, when you first come to guard, observe your opponent in this respect. Is his hand improperly placed? Does his hand drift? If so, then you have an advanced target as a probable first objective for a touch. Do not hesitate to use the point, either as a feint or after a feint with the edge. A great many fencers overreact to a feint made with the point. But don't overdo it!

Direct Attacks

The Straight Thrust. The straight thrust is usually made from tierce and seconde positions. From tierce, with the thumb and forefinger and a turning of the wrist, in pronation, the point is lowered in the direction of the thrust and the arm is then extended so that the blade and the arm form an obtuse angle. From seconde, the point is raised and the arm extended; here, the action is from the elbow.

Fencer on left makes quinte (head) parry to ward off head cut.

The Cut to the Flank from Tierce. Turn the edge of the blade from the elbow, lowering the point in the direction of the cut, and extend the arm and stretch the wrist forward completing the cut to execute a cut to the flank from tierce. In extending the arm, keep a small cutting reserve so that the completion of the cut can be made with a thrustlike movement and the stretching of the wrist. This will prohibit a pressing of the cut, a fault you should avoid.

Flank Cut from Tierce Position by an Advance and Lunge. Do not change your tierce position during the advance. Turn the fist in the direction of the cut; do not move the fist out of the horizontal plane (it should cover the arm). Extend the arm keeping a small cutting reserve and with the lunge, make the cut, stretching the wrist, for a thrust-like movement.

139

Flank cut delivered by lunge

To Execute the Flank Cut from Quinte. With the fist, turn the blade edge in the direction of the cut. Extend the arm, with the guard below the horizontal, keeping a cutting reserve. Stretch the fist forward with a thrusting movement, the guard and the point moving simultaneously.

To Execute the Flank Cut from Seconde. Raise the point to the height of the cut, extending the arm but keeping a small cutting reserve. Completion is made by stretching the fist forward to make the cut, losing the cutting reserve. Greater protection is afforded the hand, forearm, and upper arm when the point is slightly higher than the hand.

To Execute the Cut at the Right Cheek. This cut is made in much the same way as the cut to the flank. However, the blade point is raised

Presentation of blade for head cut (top) and delivery of head cut by lunge (bottom). Attack has been fully launched — hand is raised for final cut, which involves "striking" with last inch of blade.

141

to the height of the cheek, the hand is in pronation and the cut is made laterally.

To Execute the Cut at the Head from Tierce. Turn the edge of the blade in the direction of the cut, using the forefinger and thumb and a turn of the wrist. Then, extend the arm from the elbow and make the cut, again with finger and wrist action, the point sufficiently high to clear the opponent's head. During a preparation by a step forward, maintain your tierce position and present the cutting edge as you complete the step, extend the arm and make the cut with the lunge.

To Execute the Cut at the Head from Quinte. Turn the edge of the blade in the direction of the cut, and extend and lower the arm slightly below the horizontal as you make the cut.

To Execute the Cut at the Left Cheek. Turn the blade edge in the direction of the cut, again using the forefinger and thumb and a turn of the wrist; extend the arm and make the cut. The turn of the blade edge places the hand in a supinated position; the cut is made laterally. It is possible to make this cut with the back edge with the hand in pronation; this is often done.

To Execute the Cut at the Chest. This cut lands at the level of the left breast. When the cut lands in the lower line, it is known as the belly cut. The cut is made with the help of the forefinger and thumb, and the fist. The arm is extended in the direction of the cut with the flat of the blade arriving at the body first and with a slicing movement while pulling the blade back and across, it is turned over to its back edge and the cut completed. The hand is then in a pronated position and the return to tierce involves then no change in the hand position. This cut may be made with the fore edge but in recovering, it is necessary to turn the fist to the pronated position of tierce. There are valid arguments to support both ways of making this cut.

appendix a

equipment specifications[*]

GENERAL REQUIREMENTS
FOR ALL FORMS

1. The equipment and clothing of the fencer must assure the maximum protection compatible with the freedom of movement essential to fencing.
2. It must not, in any way, risk interfering with or injuring the opponent; neither may it include any buckle or opening that might, except accidentally, catch the opponent's point and thus hold or deflect it.
3. All garments must be white or of a very light tint. They must be made of sufficiently strong material and be in good condi-

---

*Reprinted by permission of the AFLA.

the on-guard position. The jacket must include an underarm lining doubling the sleeve down to the inside of the elbow (of the sword arm) and the flank in the area of the armpit. In addition, the wearing under the jacket of a protective undergarment of hemp cloth, nylon, etc., is obligatory. It must:

1. have at least two thicknesses of material.
2. include a sleeve down to the inside of the elbow (of the sword arm), without opening or seam in the area of the armpit.
3. offer the best guarantees of safety.

It may be attached to the jacket, without being entirely sewn to it.

The glove may be lightly padded.

In foil, the mask has a shape such that the bib does not come down more than two centimeters below the collar, measured when the fencer is on guard, and in any case not below the points of the collar bones (clavicles).

The clothing of women fencers includes knickers closed below the knee or a divided skirt, and, in the jacket, a breast protection of metal or some rigid material.

EQUIPMENT FOR ÉPÉE

The jacket must cover the whole of the front of the trunk, and will be completed by a lining in two parts, one doubling the sleeve down to the inside of the elbow of the sword arm, the other protecting the flank in the area of the armpit. The collar must have a minimum height of 3 centimeters. In addition, the wearing under the jacket of a protective undergarment made of hemp cloth, nylon, etc., is mandatory. It must:

1. have at least two thicknesses of material;
2. include a sleeve down to the inside of the elbow of the sword arm, and have no openings or seam in the area of the armpit;
3. offer the best guarantees of strength.

It may be attached to the jacket without being completely sewn to it.

The mask may not be covered, either wholly or in part, by a material that can make the point glance off.

EQUIPMENT FOR SABRE

1. In sabre, the masks must be well padded and furnished with bibs that are sufficiently large and strong.
2. The cuff or portion of the glove overlapping the sleeve may not be made of polished or hardened leather, or of any other material that could cause the blade to glance off.
3. The elbow protector may be made of hard leather.
4. The jacket must cover the valid surface of the trunk, with its lower part overlapping the trousers by at least 10 centimeters when the fencer is in the on-guard position.
5. The jacket must be made with a lining doubling the sleeve down to the inside of the elbow of the sword arm and the flank in the area of the armpit.

In addition, the wearing under the jacket of a protective undergarment is obligatory. It must be made of hemp cloth, nylon, etc., and must

   a) have at least two thicknesses of material;

   b) include a sleeve down to the inside of the elbow (of the sword arm), without seam or opening in the area of the armpit;

   c) offer the best guarantees of safety.

It may be attached to the jacket without being entirely sewn to it.

appendix b

field of play[*]

The field of play must present an even surface. It may not offer either an advantage or a disadvantage to either of the two competitors, particularly as regards gradient or light. In announcing a tournament, the organizers must always specify the type of surface on which the events will be fenced. They must be particularly specific when the events will be fenced in the open air.

The portion of the field of play used for fencing is called the strip ("piste"). The strip may be of earth, wood, linoleum, cork, rubber, plastic, metal, metallic mesh, or of a material with a metallic base. The width of the strip is from 1.8 to 2 meters; its length varies according to the weapon. Besides the length specified for each weapon, the strip should be extended at each end by 1.5 to 2 meters to allow the fencer who is going to cross the rear limit to retreat over an even and unbroken surface.

If the strip is placed on a platform, the latter may not be more than 0.5 meter high. If, for practical reasons, the strip cannot be of the regulation length, its length may not in any case be less than 13 meters, including the extensions mentioned above.

---

*Reprinted by permission of the AFLA.

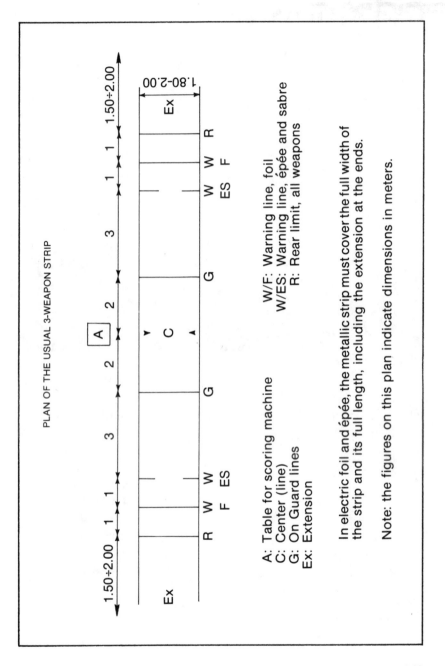

PLAN OF THE USUAL 3-WEAPON STRIP

A: Table for scoring machine
C: Center (line)
G: On Guard lines
Ex: Extension

W/F: Warning line, foil
W/ES: Warning line, épée and sabre
R: Rear limit, all weapons

In electric foil and épée, the metallic strip must cover the full width of the strip and its full length, including the extension at the ends.

Note: the figures on this plan indicate dimensions in meters.

appendix c

technical vocabulary

These are the most common terms used in judging in French, the
official language of fencing.

Prêt?	Ready?
Allez!	Fence!
Halte!	Halt!
Avertissement	Warning
La piste	The strip
L'attaque	The attack
Sur la marche	On the march
Paré	Parried
Mal paré	Insufficient parry
Après la parade	After the parry

Le Riposte	The Riposte
L'arrêt	Stop thrust
	or stop cut
Le remise	The remise
Pas valable	Off target
Pas de touche	No touch
Au bras	On the arm
Au masque	On the mask
Rien	Nothing
Trop bàs	Too low
Touché	Touched
Bon	Good
À la coquille	On the guard
Annulé	Touch annulled
À droite	Against the right
À gauche	Against the left
Coup Double	Double hit
Liemente	Bind
Mesure	Distance
Contre Temps	Counter time
Coup d'arrèt	Stop thrust
Coup de droit	Straight thrust
Degage	Disengage
Fleuret	Foil

appendix d

glossary

ABSENCE OF BLADE. A fencing situation in which the fencers' weapons are not in contact.

AIDS. The last three fingers of the weapon hand, which, with thumb and forefinger (manipulators), "aid" in finger play and dexterity of point.

ATTACK. The offensive movement designed to score a hit. May also designate the right of way.

ATTACK ON THE BLADE. A preparation of attack by beat, change-beat, pressure, froissement.

BALESTRA. A short jump forward, followed immediately by a lunge.

BARRAGE. A fence-off between two fencers who have tied in bouts won.

BEAT. A sharp, crisp, "dry" blow on the opponent's blade, opening a line or provoking a reaction. Beats are grouped under preparations of attack.

BENT-ARM ATTACK. A not fully extended arm when on the attack. It is subject to a counterattack and also to a possible ruling by the director against acquisition of right of way.

BIND (Liement). A defensive-offensive action that is a combination of two blade actions which "take" an opponent's blade from a high line diagonally to an opposite low line, or vice versa; according to the "classical" definition, the term is grouped under Preparations for Attack.

BOUT. A unit of formal competition—between two fencers in which the score is kept and entered.

BREAKING GROUND. A full step backward.

BROKEN TIME. A deliberate pause between two movements which usually follow each other immediately. The interruption of the normal or expected pattern is intended to confuse the opponent.

CADENCE. Another term for the rhythm by which a sequence of movements is made.

CEDE, CEDING PARRY. Also known as a yielding parry. Performed against a taking of the blade by a return to the appropriate guard position. Its success is dependent on yielding to the taking of the blade (bind) and returning to guard only on the final moment of the diagonal thrust.

CENTER GUARD. A foil guard position where the hand is placed in front of the body leaving outside and inside lines uncovered. This position is from the classical Italian school of fencing and rarely used.

CHANGE-BEAT. A beat made after the change of engagement.

CHANGE OF ENGAGEMENT. The action which engages an opponent's blade in a new line.

CHANGE OF LINE. The lines are disclosed by the target illustration (Chapter Three). In hand positions, we change from one line to another in attack and defense.

153

CIRCULAR OR COUNTER PARRY. A blade movement, performed by finger play and describing a circle, which picks up an opposing blade and returns it to the original line of engagement.

CLOSE QUARTERS. Also known as in-fighting. Two fencers are close to each other but still able to engage in a phrase, recognizable as such by the director.

CLOSING THE LINE. Blocking an opponent's blade movement.

COMPOUND ATTACK. An attack composed of one or more feints. Performed progressively by experienced fencers.

COMPOUND RIPOSTE. A riposte composed of one or more feints.

COQUILLE. Bell-shaped guard of either foil or épée.

CORPS-À-CORPS. Body contact between two fencers which prohibits them from further use of their weapons.

COULÉ (French term for a graze or glide). A thrust in the line of engagement maintaining contact with the opposing blade.

COUNTERATTACK. Offensive or defensive-offensive actions executed during the opponent's attack: the *stop*, a counterattack (thrust) made on an attack; the *stop with opposition*, executed while closing the line in which the opponent's attack will be terminated; the *stop in time*, made with a period of fencing time.

COUNTERRIPOSTE. Offensive action taken by a fencer who has parried a riposte.

COUNTER TIME. Describes every action made by an attacker against his opponent's stop.

COUPÉ (French term for a cut-over). A disengage made by passing *over* the opponent's blade.

COVERED, COVERING. The position taken by a defender to close a line to a straight thrust.

CROISÉ. Taking of the opponent's blade by opposing forte to foible, forcing the blade down by lowering the wrist and forearm.

CUTTING THE LINE. A parry which does not follow a normal line of defense but cuts across it, e.g., taking an attack to outside low to the inside high line.

154

DECEIVE. A move whose purpose is to evade an action by an opponent. See "feint."

DEROBEMENT. Evasion of an attack on the blade executed by the defender.

DETACHMENT PARRY. A dry, crisp beat which deflects but leaves the blade immediately after the contact.

DEVELOPMENT. A term of reference to the combination of arm extension and lunge. Does *not* include recovery to guard.

DIRECT (THRUST). A thrust that by either attack or riposte does not leave the line of engagement, as opposed to the *indirect* thrust, which does.

DIRECTOR. The official, also known as the president, who supervises the bout—the start, the halt, and the actions between—he awards the touches.

DISENGAGE. Blade movement which passes *under* an opposing blade into another line of engagement.

DOUBLE. A compound attack which deceives a circle or counterparry.

EN FINALE. To describe a parry made at the last possible moment of effectiveness.

ENGAGEMENT. When blades are in contact deliberately or unintentionally.

ENVELOPMENT. A blade taking action which, by opposing forte to foible of an opposing blade in an encircling movement, returns, and carries it back to the original line of engagement with no loss of contact.

ÉPÉE. A dueling weapon, descendant of the short sword.

FALSE ATTACK. A deliberate attacking action, apparently sincere but not intended to hit, launched rather to draw a reaction such as a parry and riposte, followed by a counterparry and counterriposte, which scores, this score being based upon an expected pattern of reaction.

FEINT. An offensive movement, apparently sincere, designed to deceive or evade an expected reaction such as a parry.

155

FENCING MEASURE. The distance between two fencers, variable according to their height and length of lunge, that is defined as the distance that enables one to score a hit on the closest target when in a full lunge.

FENCING TIME OR TEMPO, A PERIOD OF FENCING TIME. The time, variable with each fencer, required to execute one simple fencing action. The possibility of wedding two periods of fencing time into a single tempo is dependent upon speed of their execution and lies within the province and judgment of the director.

F.I.E. Fédération Internationale d'Escrime, the world governing body for the sport of fencing.

FIELD OF PLAY (Piste). The fencing strip (terrain).

FINGER PLAY. A primary characteristic of the French school of fencing featuring dexterity of point and achieved by manipulation of thumb and forefinger and the relaxation or contraction of the remaining fingers.

FLÈCHE. A running attack from out of distance, which takes the attacker past the defender on his quarte side.

FOIBLE. That half of the blade nearest to the point. This is the weaker half of the blade.

FOIL. Fencing sword with a cup guard for the hand and a thin blade, tipped with a blunt point.

FORTE. That half of the blade nearest to the guard, used to oppose the foible of the opposing blade in the execution of a parry or in the making of a thrust by opposition.

FROISSEMENT. An attack on an opposing blade made with such force as to deflect. It is grouped in the Preparations of Attack.

GAIN. The act of bringing up the rear foot to the leading foot. Used as an aid by the short fencer to compensate for his shorter lunge.

GAINING GROUND. The step forward (advance).

GLIDE. Forward movement of the blade toward target left open by uncovered guard position.

GROUND JUDGES. The two judges, one at each end, in electric foil or épée, placed so as to determine floor hits where the strip itself is not grounded so as to avoid registration when touched, or when the floor *off* the strip is touched.

HALF-CIRCLE, LOW-LINE PARRIES. Used to deflect attacks to the low line by describing a half-circle.

HIGH LINES. The target areas above the weapon hand in any guard position.

HIT. A hit or touch that is the end result of a thrust from the hand or hand and arm.

IMMEDIATE. Usually refers to the riposte delivered without a pause and therefore resulting in acquisition of right of way. The opposite of an immediate fencing movement is one that is delayed (temps perdu).

INDIRECT. An attack or riposte not delivered in the same line of engagement.

IN LINE. Refers to a position in which a fencer has his arm extended and the point threatening a valid surface. An attack made into a point "in line" must first deflect this adversary blade before acquiring right of way.

IN QUARTATA. A defensive-offensive movement, a side step, to remove the body to the side and out of the line of an on-coming blade. In its entirety, in quartata is often referred to as a "special" attack.

INSIDE LINES. The high and low target areas on the side opposite the sword arm.

INSUFFICIENT PARRY. A bad parry which does not deflect an on-coming blade from its thrust or cut to the target.

INVITATION. The opening of a line to encourage an attack—a matter of tactics.

JURY. The director (president) and judges officiating at a fencing competition.

LA BELLE. Term used for the tie-in touches—with the deciding touch yet to be decided.

LATERAL PARRY. To deflect the opponent's blade, the fencer moves his hand and blade across the body laterally.

LUNGE. The arm, leg, and body actions used to deliver a touch.

ONE-TWO. A compound attack consisting of a feint by disengage and a second disengage on the line opened by the execution of a lateral parry.

OPPOSITION. A forceful contact and pressure maintained against an adversary blade which prevents an attack or riposte from scoring. An interruption of the oncoming blade made while closing the line into which it was directed.

OUTSIDE LINES. The high and low target areas on the sword arm side.

PARRY. A defensive move made by the blade to deflect an opponent's blade. A retreat out of distance has also been referred to as a parry.

PASSATA SOTTO. An offensive-defensive movement which displaces the body by ducking under an oncoming blade; executed simultaneously with an arm extension upon which the opponent could impale himself. It has been referred to as a "special" attack.

PHRASE D'ARMES. Alternating action between attacker and defendant with correct responses that terminate with a touch, determined by the director.

POINT-IN-LINE. A basic blade position often used as a defense. The arm is extended and the point threatens a valid surface.

POOL. A tournament term used to describe a group of fencers, variable in number, assigned to a strip to compete against each other, and from which qualifiers are determined for the next round. Contestants in a pool are usually seeded, if competitive strengths of the fencers are known.

PREPARATION FOR ATTACK. Preliminary movements of foot, body or blade intended to pave or prepare the way for an attack. Present-day fencing requires a preparation prior to an attack.

PROGRESSIVE ATTACK. The correct method for executing

some compound attacks, i.e., with no pause between feint or feints and the final thrust or cut.

PRONATION. Sword hand-position with knuckles facing up.

REASSEMBLEMENT. The act of returning or bringing the leading foot back to the rear foot, and the body to an erect position.

RECOVERY, FORWARD TO GUARD. Coming to guard position forward from a lunge by bringing up the rear foot.

RECOVERY, RETURN TO GUARD. Coming back to guard after a lunge.

REDOUBLEMENT. A renewal of attack made while still in the lunge; it includes one or more blade movements.

REMISE. A renewal of attack made while in the lunge by continuing the thrust in the same line.

REPRISE. A renewal of attack preceded by a return to guard.

RIGHT OF WAY. A convention or rule of sabre and foil fencing which requires that every correctly executed attack be parried or completely evaded before the defender can maintain his own attack. The right of way is with the attack and is characterized by an extended arm threatening a valid target. However, against a point "in line," the attacker must first deflect in order to maintain his attack.

RIPOSTE. The offensive action taken by a fencer who has parried an attack.

SABRE. Sword descended from curved cavalry sabre descended from the scimitar.

SIMPLE RIPOSTE. A single blade movement, direct or indirect.

SIMULTANEOUS ACTION. The descriptive term for actions performed by both fencers, each of whom conceived and executed an attack at the same time. The touches are annulled. Must be distinguished from a "double touch" which is the result of a faulty action on the part of one fencer.

STOP HIT, STOP WITH OPPOSITION, STOP IN TIME. See Counterattacks.

STRAIGHT THRUST. An attack executed by simply extending the arm in a straight line and hitting the target from tierce or seconde.

SUPINATION. Sword hand position with fingernails facing up.

TAKING THE BLADE (PRISE DE FER). The act of taking *possession* of an opposing blade.

TROMPEMENT. A deceive performed by the attacker.

appendix e

bout procedure*

DUTIES OF THE DIRECTOR

The director will station himself at a distance from the strip that will permit him to follow the actions of the fencers thoroughly; he will follow their movements up and down the strip.

Using a microphone (preferably a wireless type) for (the finals of) official FIE competitions, he directs the bout according to the provisions of the rules.

JURY

On each side of the strip there are two judges, respectively to the

*Reprinted by permission of the AFLA.

AFIA

AMATEUR FENCERS LEAGUE OF AMERICA

OFFICIAL SCORE SHEET

EVENT _____

ROUND _____

POOL # _____ STRIP # _____

DATE _____

DIRECTOR _____

BARRAGE	#	1	2	3	4	V	hs/hr	IND	PL
	1								
	2								
	3								
	4								

CLUB	FENCER	#	1	2	3	4	5	6	7	8	V	hs/hr	IND	PL
		1												
		2												
		3												
		4												
		5												
		6												
		7												
		8												
		HS												

ORDER OF BOUTS

5 FENCERS 10 BOUTS	6 FENCERS 15 BOUTS		7 FENCERS 21 BOUTS	8 FENCERS 28 BOUTS			
1—2	1—4	6—4	1—4	3—1	2—3	8—3	3—7
3—4	2—5	1—2	2—5	4—6	1—5	6—7	4—8
5—1	3—6	3—4	3—6	7—2	7—4	4—2	2—6
2—3	5—1	5—6	7—1	3—5	6—8	8—1	3—5
5—4	4—2	2—3	5—4	1—6	1—2	7—5	1—7
1—3	3—1	1—6	2—3	2—4	3—4	3—6	4—6
2—5	6—2	4—5	6—7	7—3	5—6	2—8	8—5
4—1	5—3		5—1	6—5	8—7	5—4	7—2
3—5			4—3	1—2	4—1	6—1	1—3
4—2			6—2	4—7	5—2		
			5—7				

MULTIPLE TEAM MATES IN A POOL

POOL OF 6		POOL OF 8	
3 Team Mates *1—2—3	4 Team Mates *1—2—4—5	3 Team Mates *1—2—3	4 Team Mates *1—2—3—5

1—2	5—3	1—4	4—2	2—3	3—7	2—3	6—1
4—5	1—6	2—5	1—6	7—4	4—8	1—5	3—7
2—3	4—2	3—6	4—3	6—8	2—6	7—4	2—8
5—6	3—6	5—1	5—6	1—2	3—5	6—8	5—4
3—1	5—1	6—2	3—2	7—5	4—1	1—2	1—7
6—4	3—4	4—5	6—4	4—6	8—7	3—5	3—6
2—5	6—2	1—2	1—3	1—3	5—6	8—7	4—2
1—4		5—3		8—5	3—4	4—6	8—1
				4—2	8—1	1—3	7—5
				1—7	5—2	5—2	2—6
				3—6	6—7	4—8	8—3
				2—8	8—3	6—7	4—1
				5—4	1—5	3—4	7—2
				6—1	7—2	8—5	5—6

*Use these numbers for team mates.

Official AFLA score sheet

162

right and left of the Director, and a little behind the fencers. The two judges on the Director's right watch the fencer on the Director's left, particularly to observe the materiality of touches that may be received by that fencer. In similar fashion, the two judges on the Director's left watch the fencer on the Director's right, particularly to observe the materiality of touches that may be received by that fencer.

JUDGING
Procedure
The Director, who alone is responsible for the direction of the bouts, gives the commands. However, another member of the jury may call "Halt," but only in case of an apparent or imminent accident. Similarly, the timekeeper stops the bout by calling "Halt" at the expiration of time.

As soon as a judge sees a material touch (valid or not) against the fencer he is particularly watching, he must raise his hand to advise the Director.

All judging is carried out aloud and without the members of the jury leaving their places.

The jury is not bound by the acknowledgment of a touch by a fencer, even when properly made.

The jury first determines the materiality of the touch or touches. The Director alone then decides which fencer is touched, by applying the conventional rules for each weapon.

Materiality of the Touch
Immediately upon the stopping of the bout, the Director briefly analyzes the actions composing the last phrase d'armes before the "Halt" (this formality is not required in épée), and in the course of his analysis, he asks the two judges watching the same fencer to learn if, in their opinion, each of the actions thus analyzed by him has produced a touch against that fencer; then he does the same with the other two judges for the other fencer (these formalities are mandatory in all three weapons).

The judges, upon being questioned, must reply in one of the

following ways: "yes," "yes, but on invalid surface (off-target)," "no," or "I abstain." The Director votes last.

The Director then adds the votes thus elicited on each side; the opinion of each judge counts as one vote and the Director's own opinion as a vote and a half, with abstentions not being counted:

1. If both judges on one side agree in a definite opinion (either both "yes" or both "no," or both "yes, but on invalid surface"), their judgment prevails.

2. If one of the judges has a definite opinion and the other abstains, the Director alone can decide, since his vote is preponderant; if he also abstains, the vote of the judge having a definite opinion prevails.

3. If the two judges have definite but contradictory opinions or if they both abstain, the Director may decide according to his own opinion; if he also abstains, the touch is considered doubtful. (See paragraph 5 below.)

4. In case of a double abstention, the Director may, as an exception to the usual practice, ask the other two judges, if he believes that they were better located to see the touch—for example, when a fencer who has run past his opponent on a flèche has had a riposte aimed at his back.

5. A touch of doubtful materiality is never counted to the disadvantage of the fencer who may have received it; but, on the other hand, any touch made subsequently or simultaneously in the same phrase d'armes by the fencer who has benefited from this doubt must also be annulled; as for a touch subsequently made by the fencer who had made the doubtful touch, it is necessary to distinguish:

I.—If the new touch (remise, redoublement, or riposte) is made by the fencer who had made the doubtful touch, without any intervening touch by his opponent, this new touch must be awarded.

II.—But if the doubt was as to the place where the touch arrived (one "yes" and one "yes, but off-target"), no further touch in that phrase d'armes can be awarded.

III.—The situation is the same if, between the doubtful touch and

164

the new touch made by the same fencer, his opponent has also made a touch that has been annulled as doubtful.

Validity or Priority of the Touch

After the decision of the jury on the materiality of the touch, the Director, acting alone and by application of the rules conventional for each weapon, decides which fencer must be declared touched, or if they must both be (épée), or if no valid touch is to be awarded.

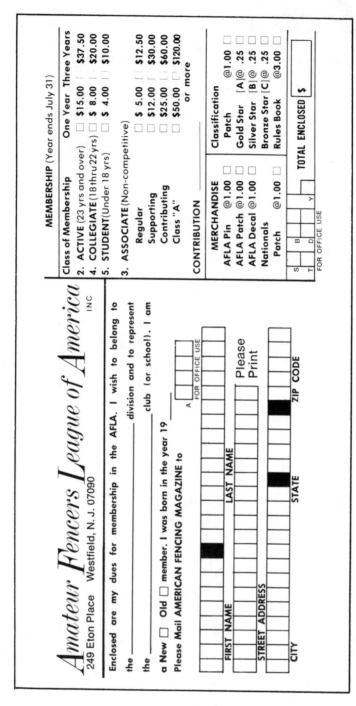

Amateur Fencers League of America INC

249 Eton Place   Westfield, N. J. 07090

Enclosed are my dues for membership in the AFLA. I wish to belong to

the _____ division and to represent

the _____ club (or school). I am

a New ☐ Old ☐ member. I was born in the year 19 ____

Please Mail AMERICAN FENCING MAGAZINE to

FOR OFFICE USE

A

FIRST NAME   LAST NAME   Please
                                               Print

STREET ADDRESS

CITY   STATE   ZIP CODE

MEMBERSHIP (Year ends July 31)

Class of Membership		One Year	Three Years
2. ACTIVE (23 yrs and over)	☐	$15.00	☐ $37.50
4. COLLEGIATE (18 thru 22 yrs)	☐	$ 8.00	☐ $20.00
5. STUDENT (Under 18 yrs)	☐	$ 4.00	☐ $10.00

3. ASSOCIATE (Non-competitive)

		One Year	Three Years
Regular	☐	$ 5.00	☐ $12.50
Supporting	☐	$12.00	☐ $30.00
Contributing	☐	$25.00	☐ $60.00
Class "A"	☐	$50.00	☐ $120.00
			or more

CONTRIBUTION

MERCHANDISE		Classification	
AFLA Pin @1.00	☐	Patch @1.00	☐
AFLA Patch @1.00	☐	Gold Star [A]@ .25	☐
AFLA Decal @1.00	☐	Silver Star [B]@ .25	☐
Nationals		Bronze Star [C]@ .25	☐
Patch @1.00	☐	Rules Book @3.00	☐

TOTAL ENCLOSED $ ____

S		B				
T		D		Y		

FOR OFFICE USE

Application for membership in the AFLA

appendix f

bibliography

Rules for Competition and *A.F.L.A. Manual*
Secretary, A.F.L.A., Inc., 249 Eton Place, Westfield, New Jersey 07090.

The Art of the Foil
Barbasetti, Luigi. New York: E. P. Dutton & Co., Inc., 1932. (Gives a short history of fencing and a rather complete treatise on the Italian school of fencing. It is out of print but available in libraries.)

Fencing: Ancient Art and Modern Sport

de Beaumont, C.-L. New York: A. S. Barnes & Co., Inc., 1960.

Your Book of Fencing
de Beaumont, C.-L. New York: Transatlantic Arts, Inc., 1969.
(This book covers Foil-Sabre-Épée with glossary of fencing terms.)

Fencing

Costello, Hugo and James. New York: The Ronald Press Co., 1962.

Fencing with the Foil

Crosnier, Roger. New York: A. S. Barnes & Co., Inc., 1951. (It is out of print but available in libraries.)

Fencing with the Sabre

Crosnier, Roger. London: Faber & Faber, Ltd., 1955.

Fencing with the Épée

Crosnier, Roger. London: Faber & Faber, Ltd., 1958.

Modern Fencing (Foil-Sabre-Épée)

Deladrier, Clovis. Annapolis: United States Naval Institute, 1948. (It is out of print but available in libraries.)

Electric Foil Fencing

Lukovich, István. Hungary: Corvina, 1971. (This translation from the Hungarian is complex and meant for the advanced fencer only.)

Escrime Moderne

Thirioux, Pierre. Paris: Éditions Amphora, 1970. (The text is in French and covers technique, tactics, teaching methods for all weapons.)

Fencing

Vince, Joseph. New York: The Ronald Press Co., 1962.

Note: Many fencing equipment suppliers carry an inventory of fencing texts. Also, whenever you are traveling about the country, try secondhand book stores. You might pick up bargains. Among many treasures of this kind is one book that is now quite valuable: *On Fencing*, by Aldo Nadi, G. P. Putnam's Sons, 1943.

appendix 9

suppliers

American Fencer's Supply Company, 2122 Fillmore Street, San Francisco, California 94115. Phone: 415-346-8662

Castello Fencing Equipment Company, Inc., 836 Broadway, New York, New York 10003. Phone: 212-473-6930

George Santelli, Inc., 412 Sixth Avenue, New York, New York 10011. Phone: 212-254-4053

Sudre Fencing Equipment Company, 5 Westwood Knoll, Ithaca, New York 14850. Phone: 607-273-2655

Joseph Vince Company, 15316 South Crenshaw Boulevard, Gardena, California 90249. Phone: 213-323-2370

Rhodes-Nishimura Engineering Company, 1122 S. Austin Boulevard, Oak Park, Illinois 60304. Phone: 312-848-9153; 312-622-1636. (*Specialty*: Sales and Repair of Electric Equipment).

index

index

index